HIGHLAND VERNACULAR BUILDING

SCOTTISH VERNACULAR BUILDINGS
WORKING GROUP

Regional and thematic studies no. 1

Edinburgh 1989

Scottish Vernacular Buildings Working Group
1989

Alexander Fenton, President
Bruce Walker, Vice President
Jane Durham, Chairman
Elspeth Dalgleish, Secretary
Sonia Hackett, Treasurer
Dorothy Kidd, Bulletin Editor
Elizabeth Beaton, Conference Secretary

Council Members
Nic Allen, Margaret McKay, Alex Muir, Anne Riches,
Ronnie Robertson, Ian Smith, Gavin Sprott, James Stewart

ISBN 0 9505084 7 0
Printed by MD Print, Edinburgh

*The cover illustration is from the M.E.M. Donaldson Collection and
is reproduced by courtesy of Inverness Museum and Art Gallery.*

CONTENTS

*This collection of essays is dedicated to
Ronald Cant D.Litt.,
friend and mentor of the
Scottish Vernacular Buildings
Working Group*

FOREWORD

There are five contributors to this book, each with his or her particular approach, yet the outcome is a sense of remarkable cohesion. Elizabeth Beaton provides a great deal of regional detail for Sutherland, Caithness and Easter Ross, both with regard to smaller scale buildings and their structural elements, and to minor lairds' houses and manses. She also looks at functional buildings like grain mills and kilns, and - as a point of especial interest - at the early use of concrete in the buildings of the Sutherland Estate, from 1871 onwards.

What she says is closely complemented by Nic Allen's material on the planned villages of the Highlands. He sets them in the context of encouragement by Government and estate owner, and shows how they were envisaged as market centres serving and supporting a rural hinterland, providing specialised trades and possibly promulgating concepts of law and order. The lining out of streets with a plough furrow is a homely touch that symbolises the way in which the lairds set up the layout, imposed regulations about building standards in their leases, and then left the hoped-for occupants to get on with putting up their own houses. They regarded public buildings, estate girnels, mills, and ecclesiastical and administrative buildings as their own prerogative, however. A gazetteer of around 50 villages for the period of 1750 - 1830 is added, with a commentary.

Bruce Walker combines the presentation of a harvest of published sources with a digest of the results of a detailed survey of buildings in the Uists. What appears is an impression of the real wealth of material that is almost on the point of vanishing altogether. In areas like the Uists, there is or was a good chance that building types and practices of pre-improvement date might be found, just as in St Kilda, as can be seen in the recent publication on the *Buildings of St Kilda* by the Royal Commission on the Ancient and Historical Monuments of Scotland. There was a time before the agricultural improvements that affected so much of Scotland, directly or indirectly, when our building traditions were much closer to those of our European neighbours; now our neighbours, through EEC regulations, are eroding even more systematically such traces as have survived.

Hugh Cheape comes to the question of horizontal water mills with a fresh eye. He demonstrates admirably the value of the linguistic element in the study of things. Probably his list of terms relating to mills is the most extensive that has ever been presented and there is little doubt, to judge by the extensive range of building terms given in Dwelly's Gaelic Dictionary alone, that a similar outcome could be expected for other kinds of buildings and their constituent elements. It is a matter of clear fact that an enormous terminology of the material culture of Gaelic Scotland is still within memory. This article highlights the urgency of recording what exists. What is lost now is lost for ever, except where captured in the words of a verse or song in fossilised form.

Malcolm Bangor-Jones presents basic source material from the eighteenth century on building work at Skelbo. Every detail of the stone and timber work is touched on. From such accounts a lost building could be reconstructed. The scale and range of the activity is impressive. We get in his introductory material an outline of those who instigated and saw to the carrying through of the work.

The variety of approaches, through history, regional variety, structural detail and language, all concentrating on the theme of buildings in the Highland parts of Scotland, is very much in line with the interests of our good friend, Dr Ronald Gordon Cant, to whom we are dedicating this small volume. His support for our Society and for societies such as ours has given a great deal of inspiration over the years. We want to show in this book that we try to respond to such inspiration. It is not our intention to review Ronald's long and active life here - it was recently done in volume 4 of *The Review of Scottish Culture* - but we wish to say to him how much he has taught us. He is himself very much aware of the new spirit that is blowing through the corridors of history. The work of the Scottish Vernacular Buildings Working Group is only a part of it, though the homes in which ordinary people lived and worked comprise a very important element of everyday existence. We wish Ronald very many more years to be our mentor, and give us the benefit of his marvellously detailed memory and of his ready willingness to advise and help us all.

Elizabeth Beaton
SOME PATTERNS IN HIGHLAND BUILDING

The keyword in Highland traditional building is variety. The purpose of this paper is to identify some regional types and to demonstrate that the pattern of traditional rural Highland secular building has many strands and textures. It is a pattern that has evolved from a wide range of building materials and building requirements, from fishing and agricultural associations to historical and geological factors; and also from ideas and influences that have made their way through glens and across sea lochs, coastal communication being of particular importance before the development of roads and railways in the nineteenth century. The evidence for this pattern survives mainly from the eighteenth, nineteenth and even early twentieth centuries, though there are indications that some types are heirs to earlier traditions. These earlier traditions include cottages with central hearths, from which the smoke seeped out through the thatch, and the "long house" in which man and beast shared common entrance and accommodation. Though such dwellings no longer exist in complete form, some of their characteristics are evident in their "improved" successors.

WEST COAST COTTAGE TYPES

The small vernacular cottage of the west, always single-storeyed and usually, though not necessarily, of symmetrical three-bay form, has broad often battered walls between 3 and 4 feet (0.91 and 1.02m) thick, bonded with clay or mud mortar. Thatch of either rushes or heather, sometimes over divots of turf, was the traditional roof covering, largely replaced by corrugated iron or slate, or now with ubiquitous proprietary materials. In the west and central Highlands the roofs of many cottages are piended (hipped), a form probably established by earlier cruck-framed "creel houses" (see below) with sloping end cruck-blades. Thatch overhangs the eaves, unlike some of the outer Hebridean cottages where the roofing joins the inner edge of the thick walls, forming a broad wallhead walk. A common characteristic is the firm securing of the roof by weighted ropes, sometimes linked around "raven sticks" projecting at the apices; this feature survives in a small single-cell cottage of early twentieth century date on Muck, where the internal space is still divided into two rooms by a roughly constructed wooden box-bed[1]. In the east, where there is a clay walling tradition, thatch was daubed with clay. Clay thatch roofs did not need to be tied down except along the eaves, weighted with a length of wood, or as at the single surviving example at Ardersier on the Moray Firth, with lengths of chain[2]. In Caithness, eaves were sometimes weighted with pieces of local flagstone known as "benlin stanes" while in north-west Sutherland crowsteps are a feature of nineteenth and early twentieth century single-storeyed cottages, a characteristic associated with earlier tower houses and larger dwellings elsewhere.

Most traditional houses in Skye have wallhead chimney stacks flanking piended roofs. These succeeded the thatched "lum" (chimney serving a central or gable hearth) which is now a rarity, though occasionally it is replaced by a drainpipe protruding through the thatch! At the time of writing only two examples of thatched lums are known to survive, both in Wester Ross: one at 27 Big Sand, Gairloch[3] and another at 12 Lower Ardelve on the northern shore of Loch Duich. The latter is a cruck-framed cottage, the cruck blades or "Highland couples" being scarf-jointed at wallhead height, fastened together with four "trenails"[4], wooden pegs with shaped heads, and neatly wall-papered where the timbers project into the rooms. Here the rush thatch is pinned with hazel wands over a divot or turf base with a fringe of heather at the wallhead to throw off the water. The eastern end flue is served by a wallhead stack, but that at the west has a traditional shaped and thatched "lum" fitted with a wooden cope; it serves the living room/kitchen hearth which has protective side cheeks and canopy, a recreation in modern materials of an original wattle or timber "hinging-lum"[5] (chimney canopy).

In Lochaber, north of a line through Loch Linnhe and Loch Sunart, occurs a three-bay plan-type with paired central hearths served by twin ridge stacks; these fireplaces warm the outer rooms, both backing on to a diminutive and cosy central chamber lit by a small rear window. There is also a two-room lobby-entry variation with a large central stack dividing the cottage with a hearth on either side. Where corrugated iron or slate replaced thatch as the covering of these hip-roofed cottages, the round battered angles have been corbelled out at the wallhead in either concrete, stone or slate in order to form the squared angles required by more rigid materials. In some cases the entire wallhead is raised with a band of concrete, providing extra internal height.

Though these traditional dwellings can be identified in Skye,

Lochaber or the central Highlands of Inverness-shire, firm typological and geographical boundaries are broken as fast as they are made. The heavily crofted southern shores of Loch Eil, for instance, reveal a rich assortment of cottages, many abandoned, some ruinous, including a perfect Skye-type dwelling. At Totaig on the south shores of Loch Duich, Ross and Cromarty, the ferry house is of the central ridge stack "Lochaber" model.

CRUCK CONSTRUCTION

Cruck construction, which transmits the roof weight more directly to the ground and allows the walls to be non-load bearing, is perfect for the substantial ventilated barns peculiar to Lochalsh, Kintail and Glenelg, where the rainfall is particularly high. These large cruck-framed barns, originally covered with heavy heather-thatched roofs, measure from 60 to over 100 feet (18.20 to 30.60m) in length and are high enough to accommodate the flail and full arm-stretch of the hand-thresher. They are usually aligned to take advantage of the prevailing wind and have wide wattled or louvred panels in the long elevations and gables, thus allowing a continuous through-draught to dry hay hung on racks and to permit the storage throughout the winter of both hay and straw, vital fodder for the black cattle that were the mainstay of the local economy. There is ample evidence that these barns were being built in the eighteenth century, probably earlier, and that they continued to be erected until the end of the nineteenth century. The ruinous seven-bay cruck-framed barn at Camus-luine in Kintail is said to have been built circa 1880, the timbers having been brought from Duncraig near Plockton; the original heather thatch survived until the building's final collapse in 1984-5 with only occasional repair by the owner[6]. Dr Johnson saw this type on Raasay in 1773 and commented that they were "so contrived because the harvest is seldom brought home dry, as by perpetual perflation to prevent the mow from heating"[7] . Nor were these barns always confined to agricultural use; the Reverend Aeneas Sage lodged in one in Lochcarron (possibly the particularly large example at Tullich, not far from the old church) before his induction as minister of that parish in 1726[8], while in 1802 James Hogg described a wedding at Ardintoul on the southern shores of Loch Duich "when we marched to the barn where the music was playing and joined with avidity in their highland reels"[9]. The rubble shell of a 70 feet (21.40m) long barn with worn cruck blades, still seated in their mural slots, stands on the loch-side at Ardintoul; a similar building near the house has an open circular

Above: 144 Oldshoremore, Kinlochbervie, Sutherland.
Below: Glendale Mill, Skye.
All illustrations in this paper are reproduced by courtesy of Historic
Buildings and Monuments Directorate, SDD.

Above: Haybarn, Kirkton of Lochalsh.
Below: Laidhay Croft Museum, Latheron, Caithness.

Cruck framed barn, Achamore, Lochalsh, with detail of scarfed joint.

horse-walk close to the entrance of the winnowing passage, "horse-power" having been used to drive the mechanical threshing drum, replacing and speeding up work previously carried out with the hand flail.

As Nic Allen and Ross Noble have shown[10], this type of construction, with wattled walls covered with turf, was widely used in some areas of the Highlands for dwellings known as "creel houses" until the very end of the eighteenth century, and indeed survived into the nineteenth[11]. In 1836 the laird of Inverie, Knoydart, lived in a house that was remarkable in as much as "the two principal rooms are finished with strong wattlework from the floor to the roof tree, for there is no ceiling (sic). The couples which support the fabric are of native fir, of great strength and size, also rising from the ground and meeting in massive arches over head . . . the whole finishing being truly Celtic, and in excellent keeping with the talents which grace its hospitable and accomplished inmates"[12]. The floor measurements and the height of the present kitchen at the rear of Inverie House suggest that it formerly contained the "principal rooms", its walls recased and no visible evidence of cruck trusses. Just possibly the crucks in the barn at Corrimony, in ·Glenurquhart, Inverness-shire, where "the cruck frames . . . are superior in size and span of their timbers, and the quality of their carpentry compared to other surviving examples in Scotland"[13] were originally in the landowner's dwelling and were relegated to agricultural use after Alexander Grant, 6th of Corrimony, erected a symmetrical two-storeyed, three-bay stone-built house in 1740, a pattern and fashion followed by other landowner-kinsmen up and down Glenurquhart in the middle of the eighteenth century.

East of Glenurquhart, on the other side of Loch Ness, the cruck frame tradition is evident in many abandoned cottages in Stratherrick, Strathnairn and Strathspey. Substantial cruck trusses from Tomatin have been re-erected at *Am Fasgadh*, the Highland Folk Museum at Kingussie, established by the pioneer expert of Scottish rural traditions, the late Dr Isobel Grant.

CAITHNESS

Cruck-framed cottages, dating from late eighteenth and nineteenth centuries, are also found in Caithness, the "Lowlands beyond the Highlands" whose rich agricultural land, herring fishing industry and abundance of excellent flagstone - but little natural woodland - have all contributed to its individual building pattern. The old croft-houses of the eastern part of the county, mainly in Latheron parish[14], are of linear form, designed to accommodate man and beast under one roof; the roof is supported by composite cruck trusses achieved by tortuous jointing of short timbers or by the re-use of boat spars, creating a characteristic rounded roofline. Some have a corn-drying kiln built into the bowed end of the barn, which, along with byre and stable, might be included in a single long building. In the north of the county the mainly nineteenth century cottages are of a more conventional three-bay type. Here larger farms have two-storeyed houses with advanced central gablets - Watten Mains dated 1763 is an excellent example - and substantial steadings with series of elegant arched cart-bays, their byres being divided with flagstone trevisses or stalls. On these farms, where considerable amounts of grain were grown and processed, large squat bottle-shaped kilns were built on to the ends of the barns to dry the corn, more grandiose than their crofting counterparts. Good examples of these large kilns survive at Hillhead and Sibster, both in Wick parish. At Sandside, Reay, there is a handsome eighteenth century kiln-barn somewhat similar to that at Rothiemay in Banffshire, and constructed in impeccable local masonry. The Innes family of Sandside originated from Banffshire, so may have been responsible for importing this alien but entirely practical design and building tradition from another grain-growing area of northern Scotland[15].

The excellence of masonry skills and local building materials coupled with extensive oat and barley crops gave rise to a series of large eighteenth and nineteenth century grain mills in Caithness, which rank amongst the finest in Scotland. All have been water-powered and have drying-kilns. At John O' Groats the large L-plan mill (1750, rebuilt 1901) has double kilns, intact machinery still water-powered, and a smaller subsidiary mill close by. At Bridge of Forss there is a handsome pair of mills, one on each side of the fast-flowing river. Achingale Mill, Watten, is also of L-plan, the rear of the building with its swept local slate roof abutting the slope which carries the lade; it has two wheels, the smaller to drive an automatic stoker feeding chaff as fuel to the kiln fire.

The flagstone quarries in the north of Caithness furnished slates for roofing, sometimes in large sections, which develop a brilliant orange colouring near the coast from the effect of algae. These flagstones were utilised in many other ways: as shelves, door and window lintels, risers and treads for staircases. On farms they are placed on end as stone fences to divide fields, they serve as stall partitions in byres and are used to make water butts and cattle troughs. One of the most important centres of the flagstone industry was at Castletown where the small harbour has a particularly wide quay to facilitate the loading of this bulky cargo on to boats for transport to Europe and even America, besides cities within the British Isles. In London the pavements of The Strand and the concourse of Euston Station were laid with these flags[16].

In Caithness, however, it was not only the flagstone trade that needed harbourage; the nineteenth century Scottish herring boom was largely centred there. Harbours such as Keiss and Sandside, both built about 1830[17], have large symmetrical three-storeyed fishing stores at the quayside and well constructed piers and breakwaters with both vertical and horizontal masonry. The small fishing station at Whaligoe (now a private house), where three hundred steps hugging the cliff-side down to the small haven were noticed by Pennant in 1769[18], and the large courtyard buildings in Wick associated with herring curing are examples at each end of the building spectrum. They demonstrate the combined effects of skilled masoncraft, excellent building materials, and sympathetic yet entirely practical designs and plan forms.

Granaries or girnals, for the storage of grain awaiting export by sea, stand on the shore at some landing places, notably at Staxigoe, which was superseded in the early nineteenth century by the larger harbour in nearby Wick. The Old Brewery in Mansons Lane, Thurso and the disused mill at Ham, Dunnet, both appear to have been early eighteenth century girnals before conversion.

EASTER ROSS

Easter Ross has coastal settlements and a rich agricultural hinterland. Many cottages in the fishing village of Inver, Shandwick, Hilton of Cadboll and nearby Fearn are of clay or clay and boulder construction. Some exhibit a rare plan-form with a through passage running from front entrance to the rear, behind a hearth warming the central chamber of a three-room dwelling; the tell-tale off-centre ridge stack indicates this unusual layout, common enough in parts of England but rare in Scotland[19]. The Easter Ross clay and boulder walling is similar to that on the south side of the Moray Firth around Speymouth; similar construction also appears to have been common in Strathspey, for when the Duke of Gordon established Kingussie about 1800, the new inhabitants were "debarred from building mud-houses"[20].

Another coastal building type that survives in unusually large numbers in Easter Ross is the estate girnal or rent house, large rectangular gabled storehouses of two and three storeys in height.

Above: Achingdale Mill, Watten. Below: East Lodge, Tarbat.

Above: Moin refuge house, Tongue. Below: icehouse, Helmsdale.

Until the early nineteenth century rents were paid in kind, largely in grain, a bulky rental that required storage depots where it could be received, and in turn from where it could be exported to realise cash. The Old Rent House at Foulis Ferry (circa 1730-40) stands on the northern shores of the Cromarty Firth, fronted by a gently sloping beach admirable for landing and loading boats, and with an assembly area to the rear for the reception of goods. At Portmahomack two of these girnals face the harbour; they were built for the Earls of Cromartie, the smaller in the 1690s and the larger in 1779. Simple slit vents provide ample through-ventilation in the bracing east coast climate. Some girnals were furnished with a fireplace served by a gable end stack, probably to keep the custodian warm, while at Foulis the doorkey is worn smooth by contact with the pocket or belt of the storekeeper[21].

MINOR LAIRDS' HOUSES AND MANSES

The success of early nineteenth century farming improvements and trade in Easter Ross is reflected in many substantial lairds' houses, some symmetrically-fronted with bowed bays and built in warm yellow, easily worked sandstone; Knockbreck near Tain is an excellent example. Where the original dwelling was of a more modest design, a later projecting bowed two-storeyed addition, housing dining and drawing rooms as at Meikle Tarrel and Geanies, indicates the later achievements and prosperity of the owner.

This pattern of substantial two-storeyed, three-bay farmhouse, minor laird's house or manse constructed from the mid-eighteenth to the mid-nineteenth century, is as common in the Highlands as elsewhere. Parish entries in both the Old and the New Statistical Accounts show how many Highland ministers were without manses up to the end of the eighteenth century, sometimes receiving a cash allowance in lieu. The "Rev. Mr. Thomas Chisholm", the ageing minister of Kilmorack, near Beauly, petitioning for such an allowance in 1767 "humbly showeth that there was no proper Manse in the said pairsh . . . the then incumbant built a kind of farmhouse of Highland Couples, with only one Room high and garrets into which your petitioner entered Anno 1712 . . . and lived there till it fell down first at one End and then the other . . . whereby he and his family . . . took shelter in an adjacent house Anno 1751"[22]. Sadly, the old man never lived to enjoy the solid two-storeyed, three-bay house erected in 1798[23], referred to as "old" in 1841[24], soon after which it was doubled in size, like so many others, by being fronted by a similarly proportioned block. There are regional manse variants, such as those of Glenelg and Glenshiel, which have piended roofs and paired ridge stacks.

LOCAL VARIATIONS OF BUILDING MATERIALS

Local building materials also make for variation of texture and pattern and are well represented in houses of the minor laird, the tacksman and the small landowner. Even if the walling is harled, the margins and dressings are of good quality polished or tooled ashlar. At Budgate in Nairnshire the five-bay symmetrically fronted eighteenth century house is of pinned or "cherry pointed" rubble masonry, small chips of local slate pressing home the mortar courses around the random rubble. A similar treatment is adapted for the harder granite of the Cairngorms. At the early to mid eighteenth century house at Clury, Duthill, the fractured ends of the regularly coursed pale grey granite are packed with contrasting darker small squares of local schist, making a decorative virtue out of necessity. In Speyside too, the rich Caledonian pine forests, in an earlier tradition the source of cruck trusses, provided ample material for internal fittings and the development of a high standard of eighteenth century house carpentry; panelled and beaded doors and window shutters, slender window astragals (glazing bars) and well turned stair balusters. These are all evident at Dell of Abernethy and Birchfield, Nethybridge, and in the old portion of Invereshie House by Kincraig. This timber was regarded as amongst the best in Scotland and formed an important source of wealth for the landowners, particularly the Grants of Rothiemurchus and of Castle Grant (later Earls of Seafield) and the Dukes of Gordon. It was floated down the River Spey to its mouth at Garmouth and Kingston-on-Spey where it was the principal raw material for the ship-building industry located there.

It is likely that many of these lairds' houses were initially slated not thatched. Besides the well known sources of roofing slate such as Ballachulish and Caithness, the use of which became more widespread in the north and north-east of Scotland after the opening of the Caledonian Canal (1822) and the expansion of the railway network (which reached Wick and Thurso by 1873 and Mallaig by 1901), smaller localised sources were exploited. Many houses in Speyside were roofed with brown-grey slates from Cnoc Fergan in Glenavon near Tomintoul, Banffshire, while similar material was quarried in Glen Banchor not far from Newtonmore[25]. Cawdor Castle, Nairn, is said to have been slated from a quarry at nearby Clava, while in the far north a silvery slate was worked at Talmine,

Melness, Sutherland, on the shores of Tongue Bay. This material was used to roof Tongue House (see below) as well as other buildings in the area, and may have travelled further afield by sea. The decaying early seventeenth century house at Skelbo Castle on Loch Fleet has been re-roofed with a similar slate.

SUTHERLAND

An important cluster of mid eighteenth century lairds' houses is located on the north Sutherland coast of the Pentland Firth, the rough waters of which formed a vital marine highway and line of communication before the development of the roads and railway. Here the Mackays of Reay and the cadet branches of their family lived in a group of small mansions that would not have shamed their counterparts further south. The House of Tongue is dated 1668, probably raised to three storeys in 1750, but with earlier core and extensive later additions: Balnakeil dates from 1744 but incorporates the foundations of the former summer residence of the medieval bishops of Caithness[26]. Bighouse at the mouth of the Halladale River also dates from mid eighteenth century, the mansion superseding an earlier diminutive U-plan two-storeyed house whose name "The Barracks" indicates its relegation to use as servants' quarters. At Bighouse there is an eighteenth century walled garden and a neat pavilion summerhouse with a weather-vane sporting the silhouette of a salmon, a sure sign that this form of fishing was a source of wealth to the estate. The salmon station at the rear of the house is still in use; the unusual early nineteenth century conical icehouse continues its original role, the ice delivered through the rear chute. This commodity now arrives by lorry from the ice factory rather than from the river and ponds whence it was formerly transported by horse and cart.

However, the dominant pattern of building in Sutherland is that of the Sutherland estate, whose massive nineteenth century reorganisation of their land and coastal resources continues to be disputed by historians and economists alike. The social upheavals in the county during the first half of the nineteenth century cannot be denied, nor can the evidence of a substantial continuous estate building programme. The established salmon stations were expanded, new icehouses with characteristic wide winged gables were built at Little Ferry, Bettyhill and Helmsdale, the latter at a cost of £100 in 1824[27](Fig.19). Helmsdale was also developed as a sea fishing station from the 1820s onwards to exploit the herring boom and to give work to crofters "cleared" from inland Kildonan;

they were housed in the neatly grid patterned village or on the outskirts in newly established crofts fronted by strip fields. The Sutherland building pattern is one of contrasts; on the one hand there are substantial farmhouses and steadings such as Inverbrora (1821), Crackaig (1829), Tongue Mains (1843) and Clynelish (1865), examples that span forty years and contrast with the crofting communities established during the same period. These are either in orderly linear plan as at Melness and Clyne, or near grid pattern at South Brora, or packed along the coast, exploiting sheltered valleys and patches of cultivable land at Skerray[28]. Peat gables and rush thatch survive at Achtoty, Strathy and Armadale on the north coast, but here, as elsewhere in the Highlands, most of the original thatched rubble cottages have been superseded by gabled single-storeyed or one and a half storeyed white-washed houses with slate roofs, constituting the emergence of another building tradition in their own right[29].

THE ERA OF CHANGE

These immense changes in the pattern of ˙Highland rural settlement, highlighted in Sutherland but evident elsewhere, combined to bring to the Highlands not only new building designs but also new building forms to accommodate new social structures and new materials with which to execute those buildings. Conversely, old skills found new uses. Thomas Telford, the principal engineer for the Commission for Highland Roads and Bridges which opened up land communications throughout the Highlands during the first two decades of the nineteenth century, found good stonemasons in Easter Ross. They utilised both their traditional drystone and mortared masonry crafts at Easter Fearn Bridge on the Struie road in about 1810, inspiring the poet Southey to comment after passing that way in 1819 that their work "form(ed) a noble display of skill and power exerted in the best manner for the most beneficial purpose"[30]. At Torgoyle in Glenmoriston Joseph Mitchell sandwiched local pinky-grey granite between dark grey schist when rebuilding in 1823, to Telford's design, the earlier bridge which had been swept away in a flood five years previously, not only completing and strengthening a very fine bridge, but making the masonry visually attractive[31]. The traditional combination bank-barns of Lochaber, with their upper threshing and storage barn floors built against a natural slope to facilitate entrance at first-floor level, and with byre and stable accommodation on the ground floor, were the basis of new steadings at Glenfinnan in

1861 designed and Gothicised by Ross and Joass of Inverness[32] and again at Arisaig by Philip Webb in 1864[33]. In these examples of bridges and barns the new has been grafted on to an already established and well proven tradition.

The early nineteenth century improved roads were augmented as lines of communication by the railways, which reached north to Wick and Thurso and west to Strome Ferry in the 1870s. The Duke of Sutherland, much of whose wealth was derived from his Staffordshire estates, was involved in the development of the railway between Inverness and Wick, being entirely responsible for the section between Golspie and Helmsdale (The Duke of Sutherland's Railway) with his private station at Dunrobin. Here the waiting room is dummy timber-framed after the manner of the English West Midland vernacular, a characteristic of some of the estate houses in Golspie and a gate-lodge designed by Andrew Maitland of Tain in 1889[34]. The latter was built for a Sutherland-born Lady Cromartie of Tarbat House at Kildary in Easter Ross, with the jettied upper storey supported by shaped brackets of smooth red Munlochy sandstone.

Another distinctive feature of Sutherland estate cottages and steadings is the gable-end skewput. Here the Scottish skewput, a stone bracket normally projecting at the front and rear corners of buildings to provide a wallhead seating for the gable skews, cope or crowsteps, has been adapted to support the English gable barge-board. One of the earliest dated examples is at Moin House erected by the Sutherland estate in 1830 as a refuge for travellers on the desolate Moin road (which the estate also built) between Lochs Hope and Tongue on the north Sutherland coast. Many of these Sutherland-type skewputs are dated, indicating that they were being constructed up to the end of the nineteenth century.

Horizontal sliding sash windows, normally quite alien to the Highlands, are also a characteristic of Sutherland estate houses.

Concrete was an innovatory building material which found popularity in the north. Some of the earliest, perhaps the earliest concrete estate buildings in Scotland, were erected between 1871 and 1881 as a series of houses, steadings, school, coach house and even dykes (field walls), designed by Samuel Barham, Master of Works to the Ardtornish estate in Morvern on the northern shores of the Sound of Mull. This land was bought and developed by one of a new breed of Highland landowners, largely made up of rich industrialists from the south, who sought leisure and sport in Scotland coupled with the prestige of a private estate[35]. Wyvis Lodge, Ross-shire (1886), was designed in a Home Counties manner, another alien style expressed in an alien building fabric. The ground floor walling is of stylised mixed random rubble and the upper floor of concrete modelled as pseudo timber framing. The building materials for the house, game and fish larders and the stables, which included the panelling and furnishings prepared in the London workshops of Walter Shoolbred, its cabinet-maker owner, were transported to the site at the extreme western end of Loch Glass by train, horse and cart and finally by boat. These shooting lodges and their ancillary buildings have become yet another stand woven into the pattern of Highland building.

ACKNOWLEDGEMENTS

The author is grateful to Dr Ronald Cant, Miss Anne Riches, Mr Geoffrey Stell and Mr David Walker for reading drafts of this paper and for their constructive and helpful comments.

REFERENCES

1   For Highland cottage construction and fittings, see I. F. Grant *Highland Folk Ways* (1961), pp.141-197. Muck cottage at NM 400800 not indicated on 2nd ed. OS, 1903, so presumably constructed after that date
2   A. Fenton "Clay Building and Clay Thatch in Scotland" *Ulster Folklife* xv-xvi (1970), pp.40-51
3   Geoffrey Stell and Elizabeth Beaton "Local Building Traditions" Donald Omand (ed.) *The Ross and Cromarty Book* (1984), p.209
4   *New Statistical Account* vol 14 (1836), p.196
5   For further information on 12 Lower Ardelve, see James R. Sounness "Re-thatching at 12 Lower Ardelve, Lochalsh", *Vernacular Building* vol 10 (1986), pp.17-24; Sheila Mackay (ed.) *Scottish Victorian Interiors* (1986)
6   Pers. comm. February, 1985. Mr Duncan Matheson ("The Stalker") Camus-luinie, Kintail. James Robertson *General View of Agriculture of the County of Inverness* (1808), p.193
7   Samuel Johnson *A Journey to the Western Islands of Scotland* R. W. Chapman (ed.) (1924), p.72
8   Donald Sage *Memorabilia Domestica* (1899), p.4-5
9   James Hogg *Highland Tours* William F. Laughlan (ed.) 1981, p.84
10   N. G. Allen, "Walling Materials in the eighteenth century Highlands" *Vernacular Building* vol 5 (1979), pp.1-7; R. Ross Noble "Turf-walled Houses of the Central Highlands" *Folk Life* vol 22

(1983-84), pp.68-83

11   James Robertson *op.cit.* p.58

12   *New Statistical Account* vol 14 (1836), p.135

13   Geoffrey Hay "Corrimony Barn" *Scottish Studies* vol 17 (1973), pp.127-133

14   Geoffrey Stell and Donald Omand *The Caithness Croft* (1976). Also Geoffrey Stell "Some Small Farms and Cottages in Latheron Parish" J. R. Baldwin (ed.), Caithness, *A Cultural Crossroads* (1982), pp.86-115

15   Elizabeth Beaton "The Sandside Kilnbarn" *Caithness Field Club Bulletin* Spring 1988

16   Donald Omand and John Porter *The Flagstone Industry in Caithness* (1981); J. R. Baldwin (ed.) *op.cit.* (1982), John Porter "An Introduction to the Caithness Flagstone Industry", pp.115-129

17   John Hume *The Industrial Archaeology of Scotland* vol 2 (1977), pp.194,199

18   Thomas Pennant *A Tour in Scotland in 1769* (1774), p.334

19   Bruce Walker "Notes on Cottages with Cross Passages in Inver, Tain, Ross-shire" *Vernacular Building* vol 4 (1978), pp.28-30

20   James Robertson *op.cit.* p.70

21   Elizabeth Beaton "Late Seventeenth and Eighteenth Century Estate Girnals in Easter Ross and South-east Sutherland", J. R. Baldwin (ed.), *Firthlands of Ross and Sutherland* (1986), pp.133-149. For Portmahomack girnal see Monica Clough, "The Cromartie Estate, 1660-1784: Aspects of Trade and Organisation", also in J. R. Baldwin *op.cit.* (1986), p.93

22   Scottish Record Office E769/103/2

23   *Statistical Account* vol 20 (1798), p.408

24   *New Statistical Account* vol 14 (1841), p.370

25   Information by courtesy Mr Ross Noble, Highland Folk Museum, Kingussie.

26   David MacGibbon and Thomas Ross *The Castellated and Domestic Architecture of Scotland* vol 4 (1892), pp.80-81

27   National Library of Scotland, Sutherland Papers, Dept. 313/111/Box 24.

28   For Skerray see James B. Caird, "The Making of the North Sutherland Crofting Landscape in the Skerray District" Alex Morrison (ed.), *North Sutherland Studies* (1987), pp.38-53

29   Elizabeth Beaton "Notes on some Building Types and Traditions in Tongue and Farr Parishes" Alex Morrison (ed.), *op.cit.* (1987), pp.68-70

30   A. R. B. Haldane *New Ways through the Glens* (1962), pp.69

31   *Ibid.* pp.130,163,171

32   *Inverness Advertiser* June 18, 1861
33   Roger Dixon and Stefan Muthesius   *Victorian Architecture* (1978), p.269
34   *Inverness Courier* February 22, 1889
35   Philip Gaskell *Morvern Transformed* (1968), pp.57-63

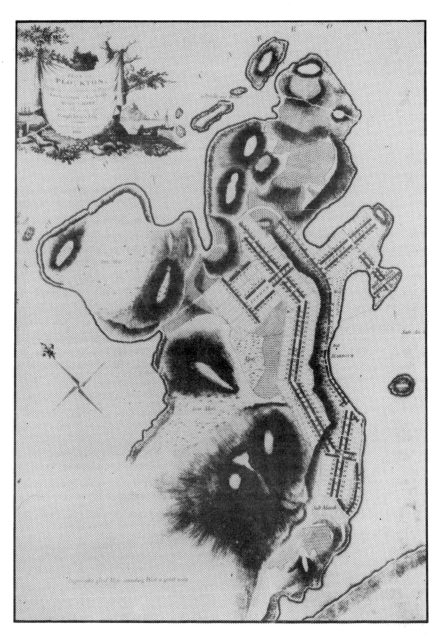

Plan for Plockton by William Cumming, 1801 (Copy of print held by National Trust for Scotland, Balmacara).

Nic Allen

HIGHLAND PLANNED VILLAGES

"I should be very well satisfied if in my lifetime I could make anything like a town in one part of my estate."

Sir James Macdonald of Sleat 1769[1]

THE IDEA OF THE VILLAGE

A remarkable variety of people took an interest in the economic development of the Highlands during the late eighteenth century. And equally remarkable is the extent to which they agreed upon the need for a single catalyst in bringing about such development. That catalyst was the village or town and since such forms of settlement were virtually unknown in the Highlands at that period, the solution lay in establishing brand new villages.

It was a theme taken up by economists, agricultural writers - every one of the Board of Agriculture sponsored county surveys for the Highlands and Islands, published from the 1790s, mentiona the importance of new settlements[2] - and parish ministers alike. The Statistical Account was dotted with references to the desirability of village foundation. No fewer than half the parish ministers of Sutherland, for instance, enthused about such possibilities[3]. The minister of Lochcarron quite literally waxed lyrical on the subject, writing:

"In Humbay there's a harbour fine
  Where ships their course may steer
  Such as are building villages
  Might build a village here"[4]

The response was as enthusiastic as the call. Between 1750 and 1830 government or quasi-governmental organisations such as the Annexed Estates Commissioners and the Board of Manufactures, privately funded companies such as the British Fisheries Society[5] and every one of the great landowning families of the Highlands - Sutherland, Mackenzie of Seaforth, Macdonald of Sleat, MacLeod of Dunvegan, Clanranald, Cameron of Locheil, Grant of Grant and the Dukes of Gordon - and numerous minor ones, set in motion the establishment of almost fifty new Highland settlements[6].

Town planning in the Highlands, as its eighteenth century propagandists were well aware[7], had much earlier origins. An Act of 1597 "Anent the bigging of Burrowes Townes in the Isles and Hielandis" facilitated the establishment of Campbeltown, Gordonsburgh (later renamed Fort William) and Stornoway. The motive here, as in the almost contemporaneous Jamesian plantations in Ulster, was a clear and an ageless one. From the *bastides* of medieval France to the Fortified Hamlets of twentieth century Malaya and Vietnam, the village or town has been seen as the focal point of central government authority in a hostile rural environment. A century and a half after the 1597 Act, James Small, the Annexed Estates factor on the Struan estate summed it up perfectly when, in recommending Kinloch Rannoch as a location for a settlement, he noted it was "the most centrical part in this corner of the Highlands for a prison, a Magistrate and a minister of the gospel"[8].

A keystone in such a policy was the introduction of a population loyal to central government authority. Again Highland experience mirrors that of Ulster. Lowlanders populated Kintyre as they did north-east Ireland. The Fife Adventurers were given responsibility for Stornoway in much the same way as Londonderry became the fiefdom of the London Guildsmen. In the 1760s classically minded Commissioners of the Annexed Estates looked further back in history, and taking the example of the Roman settlements of ex-soldiers (*coloniae*), planted veterans of the Seven Years Wars in the Highlands[9].

But securing law and order was never an end in itself. In 1771 the Annexed Estates Commissioners were instructed to "have a particular attention . . . to the enlargement, or new erection of towns and villages, to the end that the inhabitants by neighbourhood and mutual commerce, may be better enabled to assist each other in agriculture and in securing their property against theft and rapine"[10]. Security and commerce were, after all, simply the two sides of the single coin of Georgian civilisation.

Even this attitude was something of an anachronism by the 1770s. Government backed schemes of the 1750s and 1760s may have stressed the role of towns and villages in securing law and order; the private schemes which followed were almost wholly concerned with the economic benefits of settlement foundation. The Scottish Establishment was now more gripped by the theories of Adam Smith than by fears of Jacobitism. And if Smith propounded the view that division of labour with its attendant market benefits was the prerogative of an urban society - "In the lone houses . . . which are scattered about . . . the Highlands of Scotland, any farmer must be butcher, baker and brewer for his own family"[11] - he was no more than stating what, by then, had become the general economic doctrine among his contemporaries.

"It is almost unnecessary to observe", wrote the minister of North Uist, that "erecting villages would help much to better the condition of the people as then the tenant would be furnished with the market at hand for many articles that now turn to no account."[12] The Agricultural Survey of Inverness asked rhetorically "where does every commodity of food and clothing yield the best possible price? On those estates where collective bodies of men are settled together."[13] The symbiotic relationship between market centre and rural hinterland was stressed by Cosmo Falconer, early nineteenth century factor on the Sutherland estate, who wrote that farms in the proximity of a village would find a market for "even those articles at present considered of trifling consequence"[14]. Peter Fairbairn, Mackenzie of Seaforth's secretary, noted "the mutual advantage and convenience that visibly should arise to the country and townspeople" by the establishment of a market day in Stornoway[15], and the author of the Agricultural Survey of the Hebrides, stressing the indebtedness of country to town in this matter, asked "what would Bute be without Rothesay, Lewis without Stornoway, or the Isle of Man without Douglas and its other towns? What an honour to Islay and to Mr Campbell of Shawfield are Bowmore, Portnahaven and to Mr McLean of Coll his thriving establishment on the north of Mull."[16]

John Anderson, later to become factor on the Gordon estate, introduced another element. Writing from Badenoch in the 1790s, he noted that "there is no village, either in the parish or in the whole district. This inconvenience is severely felt. Not only the luxuries, but even many of the common necessities of life must be sent to a distance of more than forty miles. Tradesmen have no fixed place of residence where they can be resorted to. There is no centre for the little traffic or barter requisite to be carried on in an inland country."[17] The lack of specialised trades was an inevitable result of the lack of markets as the Agricultural Survey of the Hebrides noted, "the present want of labourers, of mechanics, of industry and consequently of many of the first comforts of civilised society must be imputed to the scarcity of villages and the total want of towns."[18]

The call then was for urbanisation and this is reflected in the nature of the new settlements that sprang up around the

Highlands. In England at this time landlords were gathering day labourers and artisans servicing the needs of their estates into quaint "model" or "estate" villages. The Highland proprietor, on the other hand, saw his villages as the cradle of industry and commerce. Both groups indulged in fantasies but they were of a very different kind. The model village was the recreation of a rural idyll. The Highland planned village was no less than a nascent town.

THE PROCESS OF FOUNDATION

Between the acceptance of the economic rationale for village foundation and its fulfilment, lay the process of choosing a site, laying out the settlement, attracting a population and building and regulating the village.

Choice of site was governed by the availability in the location of building materials, fuel, improvable land, fresh water and, above all - given the rationale for establishing villages in the first place - suitability in terms of providing ease of access to the largest possible population.

In his advice to the British Fisheries Society in 1787, Sir James Grant of Grant summarised the business of laying out a village. Grant was an eminently practical planner, and by this date had many years of experience in village establishment at Grantown and Lewiston behind him, so his blueprint is worth quoting at length:

"I imagine", he wrote, "it may be proper at the first establishment to line out the intended town upon a regular plan according to the characteristic situation of the ground that the streets may be rectangular and convenient, and the market place, the storehouse, wharfs, granaries, quay, and pier placed in the most advantageous manner, the public roads of the adjacent country should likewise be brought through the town, and a charter obtained for holding a certain number of fairs in the year and a weekly market in each village to induce the inhabitants of the country adjoining to bring in provisions, clothing, fuel etc. and to render it as much as possible the rendezvous of all the public meetings.

To render the village immediately agreeable and comfortable for strangers, I should think a principal Inn and an inferior one should without loss of time be erected by the Society and set to proper people - I would likewise build houses for a baker and brewer, a smith, a carpenter and a mason as being people immediately necessary to all settlers - a good school should also be established by the Society and encouragement given to one or more good motherly women for training the young children from 4 or 5 years of age to virtue and industry, teaching them their catechism, knitting of stockings etc.etc. This last is highly agreeable to the country people and will tend much to entice them to settle in or near the village.

Having lined out the key or harbour, the market place and different streets it will be proper to mark off the different tenements or lots for building allowing room for the necessary offices behind the house and a small garden equal to the consumption of the family perhaps a lot or tenement of from 50 to 60 feet in front, and from 300 to 350 feet in length backwards may answer, or about the fourth of a Scots acre in whole. The lot or tenement should be the undoubted property of the person who takes it, holding in feu of the proprietor of the neighbouring land or of the company, and as parchments and charters occasion intricacy and trouble, and expense to poor people, I rather think that feu letters or long leases are more eligible.

Besides the above buildings which may be necessary the Society should interfere as little as possible with building. It will inevitably bring them into a great deal of useless expense, many of the houses may be uninhabited, and those that are inhabited will not be taken near so much care of or so much enjoyed as those which they build for themselves.

Such as cannot build and make gardens at their own expense should have an advance of money sufficient to assist them upon proper conditions of repayment, which should be punctually insisted upon, . . .

I imagine it may be necessary to give those who shall settle in the villages to be erected, 2 acres of ground to each fisher . . .

It may be thought expedient to secure in feu or long lease arable and improveable lands in the vicinity of each village to the extent of 4 or 500 acres."[19]

Most of the suggestions made by Grant were adhered to in principle if not in practice by his contemporaries.

Thus those whose ambitions ran to more than a single street village almost invariably adopted the "rectangular", right angled, street pattern recommended by Sir James. A plough was listed among the earliest cargos of building materials shipped to Ullapool in June 1788 and by Autumn of that year the first streets were being lined out "with a plough furrow"[20]. The lining out of the streets in this manner was commonplace and, like the *coloniae* concept, appealed to the classically trained eighteenth century mind. As an excited James Macdonald wrote of Portree in 1783: "I have had the whole marked with a plough that the city may be founded in the true classical way. All the gardens and enclosures are also marked so that I have already a complete view of the work."[21]

Plans - drawn, more often than not, by the ubiquitous north-eastern land surveyors[22] - were important, not only to guide the lining out of streets, but also as an essential reference to holdings in the new village. This was particularly important when a local agent was having to liaise with a proprietor or factor at some distance. Thus, James Grant, writing from Castle Grant to the planner of Lewiston, insisted that "as soon as you have marked out the whole [village] in such a way as not to admit of mistakes, you will make Mr Willox [the Urquhart factor] master of it, and let him have the tenements numbered so that by letters he can let me know what tenement is offered for, and I can give him my answer from the plan you give me."[23]

The availability of land in Lewiston was brought to the local population's attention "at the Kirk of Urquhart on two or three Sundays"[24], and making proposals for a village known locally cannot have presented many problems. More difficult was attracting the attention of those outside the immediate vicinity whose specialist skills made them such attractive potential settlers. The method adopted by the majority of Highland proprietors was newspaper advertising. In the eighteenth century, it was usual to choose one or both of the major Edinburgh newspapers - the *Caledonian Mercury* and the *Edinburgh Evening Courant* - but the *Aberdeen Journal* was also recommended[25] and used particularly in the case of central Highland villages. The monopoly enjoyed by these newspapers was challenged by the establishment in 1807 of the *Inverness Journal.*

Only in the case of more ambitious projects did proprietors look further afield. Helmsdale, for instance, was advertised in the newspapers of Dundee, Leith and Berwick upon Tweed[26] and with grandiose plans for Kyleakin, no expense was spared. In 1811, 300 copies of plans drawn up by the estate's egregious architect, James Gillespie, were sent to Inverness, Peterhead, Greenock, Edinburgh, Belfast, Liverpool and London, as well as to a number of landowners in Scotland[27].

More realistic inducements to would-be settlers included the building stance, a garden and, quite often, a smallholding situated, as the layout of the village allowed, either behind the garden or outside the settlement. Smallholdings were invariably held on relatively short leases; arrangements regarding building stances were more controversial and represented one of the few examples of the views of the propagandists sometimes conflicting with those of the planners. James Robertson in the Inverness Agricultural Survey, insisted that those proprietors who were prepared to grant feus would see their settlements "leave the other villages far behind and daily outstrip them more and more in population, in ornament, in industry, in the urbanity of the people and in every desirable object."[28] James Macdonald, in the Hebridean Survey agreed "it is independence and independence alone which can make amends for the inclemency of climates and the barrenness of soils[29].

Macdonald's namesake on Skye, on the other hand, represented the conservative norm among the landowners on this point: "These people always want to get feus" he complained in 1763, "which I do not choose to grant. But any lease I would grant without scruple."[30] This was, in fact, an understandable prejudice in an era when the feuing of even small plots within a Highland estate was a complete novelty. What was, in fact, more remarkable than Sir James's disinclination, is that there were those among succeeding generations of landowners who did come round to the idea of feuing. Indeed, references to feus on a Highland estate at this period are a sure indicator of the presence of a planned village. For the most part, however, long leases continued to be the norm; 99 years, for instance, being considered the "usual duration" by William Young on the Sutherland estate[31].

Whether the building plots were feued or leased, proprietors were often prepared to offer *douceurs* to encourage development. On the Gordon estates, for instance, it was agreed that so "that the industrious poor may not be crippled in their exertions to build decent houses, an adequate feu duty ought to be preferred to entry money" and in the case of Kingussie, even the payment of feu duties was overlooked during the first three years of possesion, in order to defray building costs[32]. Similarly, in Sutherland, James Loch noted that the standard rental for villagers of Helmsdale had been fixed at "two shillings for the first ten years of a 99 year lease, five shillings for the next ten years, ten shillings for the third ten years and 20 percent for the residue. This rate is very moderate but it will induce settlers to fix themselves . . . It promises a good rent and will procure the most lasting and permanent advantages to the estate."[33]

There was another, particularly tempting, inducement which could be offered to settlers. As a surveyor on the Macdonald estate noted, "a piece of good land behind his house I have always found to be the greatest temptation that could be held out to a poor settler."[34] It was a temptation, too, for the landowner. A piece of land lying near the village would not only provide the villager with subsistence when other means failed - a particularly important point in the case of fishing villages whose livelihood was naturally subject to fluctuations - but would also bring the landlord more rent, and, it was hoped, improve the quality of the land. John Blackadder, surveying the Macdonald of Sleat estates, suggested, for instance, that settlers at Kyleakin need pay no rent for their smallholdings in their first four years of possession, but would be removed if they had not improved the land during that period[35].

There was, however, one very grave danger in holding out such an inducement; it could undermine the whole rationale for creating villages in the first place. As Cosmo Falconer put it, "a farmer fisher is a kind of heterogeneous jumble that ought to be separated. Their whole attention should be directed and kept in its proper sphere of action. The same holds good with weavers, tailors, manufacturers, etc., or the proper division of labour cannot be accomplished if they are not obliged to depend on, and follow out, the different occupations allotted to them for support. A small portion of ground for a garden is the utmost that should be allowed."[36]

It was a problem which the gloomier commentators saw as a fatal flaw in the whole business of village planning. As Alexander McLean of Coll declared succinctly in his comments to the British Fisheries Society, "Tradesmen of all descriptions are not to be got without procuring farms for them or some proportion of land and, no sooner is this procured, than they become farmers solely and give up their trade."[37] Interestingly enough, it was to be one of the Society's villages which very much proved just this point. At Lochbay on Skye, where the villagers were granted relatively good quality holdings, they had, as early as 1797, just five years after the establishment of the village, abandoned fishing for farming[38]. In 1808 it was reported that "if they can but bring themselves through at all by the produce of their acres, they have no ambition for changing their manner"[39].

VILLAGE BUILDINGS

The urban aspirations of Highland planners were particularly well illustrated by their approach to building operations. Village buildings were, for the most part, simple and functional. Where they did aspire to any architectural pretension, it was of the hard, neo-classical, urban variety. Even where building proposals became absurd, as they did at Gillespie's Kyleakin or Telford's Lochbay, it was the thoroughly urban absurdity of Georgian terraces and crescents straggling across the peat hags of Skye rather than the absurdity of the rural idyll - *cottages ornées* and Gothyke dairies - which we associate with the planned estate villages of the south.

Another corollary of the urban model ensured that such Georgian follies were never built. The Highland villages were planned as centres of commerce and industry, not of rural paternalism, and proprietors were always reluctant to undertake themselves the building of houses for the inhabitants.

Those charged with the practical headache of actually attracting settlers into new settlements - surveyors like John Blackadder[40] on Skye, or factors such as Alexander Shaw and John Willox on the Grant estates - had their own reasons for encouraging a more flexible approach. In the late 1760s when Lewiston was being planned, Shaw urged the estate to build a few houses "to induce strangers to come" and Willox backed this up: "The country people are so ignorant that they cannot be prevailed on to begin till they see some person build before them." The estate, however, remained unresponsive[41].

Proprietorial influence on the pattern of domestic building in the villages was, therefore, generally confined to what could be exercised through building regulations contained in leases or feus. These were generally interpreted in a fairly liberal fashion. "From the poverty of the people", wrote a factor on the Macdonald estate in 1800, "they cannot possibly lay out much money at the commencement, and if the rules and regulations were strict, they could not be brought to settle in villages at all."[42]

In fact, the principal concern of village founders was simply to ensure that houses were set down in conformity with the overall plan. "Villagers at Helmsdale", James Loch wrote, "must not encroach on the lines of the street, but they may build up to it or back from it, with one storey or two just as they fancy."[43]

A common regulation related to building materials. At Lewiston in 1770, villagers were to build "small, neat, stone houses within two or three years after their settlement"[44]. A feu charter of 1807 for Kingussie called for houses to be "all of stone and lime or of stone and clay sufficiently pinned with lime on the outside"[45]. In 1818, Francis Suther, the Sutherland factor, ordered the houses of Helmsdale "to be built with stone and lime and covered with gray slate or tiles"[46]. The inclusion of such clauses in leases was not confined to new villages. In fact, it was quite common practice in general on Highland estates of the period[47]. However, the feus and excellent leases granted to villagers probably encouraged rather

Print showing James Gillespie's 1811 scheme for Kyleakin.

better building standards in the settlements than elsewhere. Certainly the Agricultural Survey of Inverness specifically commented on the pleasing state of Kingussie, which it attributed to regulations forbidding the building of "mud houses"[48].

Public buildings, on the other hand, were very much part of the proprietors' responsibilities. The village inn, to which, as centre of market activities, great importance was attached, fell firmly into this category. The wealthier village planners built new inns within the settlements as, for instance, at Ullapool, Lochbay, Brora, Helmsdale, Port Gower and Kyleakin. Elsewhere, inns in the vicinity of a village, as at Pitmain for Kingussie and Drumnadrochit for Lewiston, were improved and in some villages tenants were encouraged to improve inns and change houses which already existed within settlements, as at Gordonsburgh.

The encouragement of industry required proprietors to build, where appropriate, jetties, storehouses and mills, as well as encouraging others to do so. Accommodation was needed (and tended to be the proprietor's concern) not just for those involved in village administration, but also government employees such as customs officers at Ullapool and Stornoway, and the fishery officer at Kyleakin, whose presence so facilitated local enterprise.

Finally, there were the ecclesiastical and administrative buildings - another proprietorial responsibility. Village sites seldom coincided with the location of existing parish churches, but with the establishment of *Quod Sacra* parishes to cope with growing populations, several planned villages such as Plockton and Shieldaig were equipped with the ubiquitous Telford-designed church and manse. In some cases, too, new villages as local centres of population were chosen as the location for new administrative buildings. The courthouses of Kingussie and Portree, for instance, are amongst the grandest buildings in the settlements.

REFERENCES

1   National Library of Scotland Macdonald of Sleat MS1309 f238 Macdonald to Mackenzie 17 Aug 1763
2   Agricultural Surveys: J. Macdonald *Hebrides* (1811) pp.70-71, J. Robertson *Inverness* (1808) pp.xxiii-xxiv, J. Henderson *Sutherland* (1812) p.158, J. Smith *Argyle* (1798) p.308, G. S.Mackenzie *Ross and Cromarty* (1813) p.243
3   *Statistical Account* vol 3 (1791) p.519; vol 6 (1790-1791) pp.291, 317n; vol 10 (1793) p.301; vol 16 (1794) p.210; vol 21 (1790-1791) p.227

4   *Statistical Account* vol 13 (1793) p.560
5   For details of the village founding work of these
organisations see A. Smith *Jacobite Estates of the Forty Five* (1982),
A. S. Cowper *Linen in the Highlands* (1969) and J. Dunlop *British
Fisheries Society* (1978)
6   This paper is concerned with the area covered by the present
day Local Authorities of *Comhairle nan Eilean* and Highland Region
(excluding the lowland areas of the eastern seaboard). A general
introduction to village planning in Scotland as a whole is to be
found in T. C. Smout "The Landowner and the Planned Village in
Scotland" 1730-1830 pp.73-106 in N. T. Phillipson and R. Mitchison
(ed.) *Scotland in the Age of Improvement* (1970)
7   J. Knox *View of the British Empire* (1785) pp.163-64
8   Scottish Record Office E783/84/111
9   see T. C. Smout (1970) p.90
10   SRO E730/32
11   A. Smith *Wealth of Nations* (1776) vol i, p.21
12   *Statistical Account* vol 13 (1793) p.325
13   J. Robertson p.354
14   R. J. Adam *Sutherland Estate Management* (1972) vol i, p.29
15   SRO Seaforth GD46/17/15 Fairbairn to Seaforth
16   J. Macdonald
17   *Statistical Account* vol 3 (1790) p.38
18   J. Macdonald p.70
19   SRO British Fisheries Society GD9/3 pp.105-107
20   SRO GD9/3 p.151, GD9/4 p.63
21   NLS MS 1309 f254-256 Macdonald to Mackenzie 23 Oct 1763
22   For details of these important men see I. Adams *Peter May*
(1979). Those involved in Highland village planning included
Peter May, George Brown and William Cumming (see details in
Gazetteer)
23   SRO Seafield GD248/677/1 p.5 Grant to Taylor 3 Jan 1770
24   SRO GD248/242 "Memoir as to the intended village at
Kilmore Oct 1769"
25   SRO GD9/159/4 Macleod to Porter 19 Apr 1802
26   Stafford County Record Office D593/K1/5/7 Loch to Suther 13
Jan 1818
27   See entry for KYLEAKIN in Gazetteer
28   J. Robertson p.71
29   J. Macdonald pp.70,770
30   NLS MS 1309 f238 Macdonald to Mackenzie 17 Aug 1763
31   R. J. Adam vol i, p.134
32   SRO Gordon GD44/28/35 John Anderson's Report Dec 1806;

J. Robertson p.70

33   SCRO D593/7L/2/1 Report on the English and Scottish Estates Sept 1818 p.120

34   SRO Macdonald GD221/98 Diary Jun-July 1799

35   *ibid*

36   R. J. Adam vol i, p.27

37   SRO GD9/3 p.90

38   SRO GD9/132 Robertson's Report p.5

39   SRO GD9/196/5 Grant to Salton 14 Nov 1808

40   SRO RH2/8/24 Survey of Skye and N Uist 1799, p.133

41   GD248/49/3/1 Shaw to Grant 26 Jan 1767; GD248/242 Willox to Grant 2 Dec 1769 and 12 Mar 1770

42   SRO GD221/63/63 Campbell to Campbell 3 Jan 1800

43   SCRO D593/K/1/5/6 Loch to Suther 25 Dec 1817

44   SRO GD248/677/1 p.5 Grant to Willox [Jan 1770]

45   SRO GD44/28/21 feu charter of John Anderson 24 Mar 1807

46   SCRO G593/K/1/3/6 Suther to Loch 17 May 1818

47   See N. G. Allen "Building and Walling Materials in the eighteenth century Highlands" in *Vernacular Building* vol 5 (1979) pp.1-7

48   J. Robertson p.70

GAZETTEER OF HIGHLAND PLANNED VILLAGES

This gazetteer is set out by village, parish and county and, on the next line, the name of the proprietor. Information is provided in a shorthand form and holdings and their locations relate to the above noted references. Any extant village plans are noted at the end of each entry.

ARISAIG or ARDNATUARAN *Arisaig, Inv*
Clanranald
To be laid out in eight principal lots. "It is proposed that new houses should be built on the road-side" (GD201/5/1217/28   Report by Robert Brown Jun 1798; GD201/5/1233/29 Tutors Minutes 12 Jun 1798 pp.5-6)

ARNISDALE *Glenelg, Inv*
Stevenson of Oban

AIROR or 'BALLY-BHEY-AC' *Glenelg, Inv*
Macdonell of Glengarry
Leases of 50 years to be granted. Plans to be drawn up by James
Gillespie (*Inverness Journal* 22 Aug 1817)

BRORA *Clyne, Suth*
Sutherland
Laid out from 1811, 99 year leases granted (J Loch *Acount of the
Improvements* 1820 pp.134,160-162)
Plans - William Forbes 1811-13 (Loch pl.7)

BUNDALLOCH *Kintail, Ross*
Mackenzie of Seaforth
Survey for village commissioned from William Cumming (GD46/17/
19 "Report to Lord Seaforth" Apr 1801).
See also DORNIE

CARRBRIDGE *Duthil, Inv*
Grant of Grant
Reference to "terms on which the houses at Bridge of Carr are to be
built" (GD248/1551 letter to John Sim, land surveyor 27 Nov 1808)

CASTLEBAY *Barra, Inv*
Macneil of Barra
Macneil states "my intention to erect at Ardglass at Castletown a
fishing village consisting of seventy small houses or
thereabouts" (SRO SC29/64/6 7 Feb 1825). Accounts for work on
village (*ibid*). Factor sent to Lewis to find tenants for village
(GD46/17/70 Macneil to [Seaforth or Adam] 6 Nov 1826)

CORPACH *Kilmallie, Inv*
Cameron of Lochiel
"If the Caledonian Canal shall succeed, and that Lochiel adheres to
his resolution of erecting a village at Corpach at the mouth of the
Canal, it may probably turn out a formidable vival to the town of
Gordonsburgh" (GD44/25/8/88 "Memorial respecting the set of the
Duke of Gordons Lochaber Estate" 1805 p.9)

CULGOWER *Loth, Suth*
Sutherland
Fishing village suggested in 1803 (R. J. Adam, *Sutherland Estate
Management* (1972) vol 1, p.xxxii-iii)
Plans drawn up by David Wilson (Sutherland Factors Accts &

Vouchers 1807/14)

DORNIE *Kintail, Ross*
Mackenzie of Seaforth
Plans drawn up by David Urquhart (GD46/17/3 Fairbairn to Seaforth 1 Mar 1794. See also PLOCKTON) Settlers have problems finding wood for their buildings (GD46/17/14 "Memorandum for Lord Seaforth" 6 Mar 1799). New survey made by William Cumming (GD46/17/19 "Report to Lord Seaforth" Apr 1801). "The thriving town or village of Dornie . . . founded only a few years ago, has a population of from 400 to 500 inhabitant . . . now exceed[s], in most respects, any of the villages settled or fostered by the British [Fisheries] Society, although it has been left entirely to the exertions and perseverance of the inhabitants" (*Inverness Journal* 20 Mar 1812). See also A. Mackenzie "Dornie and its Antiquities" in *Transactions of the Inverness Scientific Society* vol 4, 1891 pp.108-110

GLENELG *Glenelg, Inv*
Macleod of Dunvegan
Site for village to be identified by George Brown (Macleod Papers, box 51 "Notes respecting a Survey of McLeods Estate" [1787 or 1788]). Village buildings erected by 1788 (GD9/3 p.61). "If a manufacture for coarse cloths on a small scale was established in a village lately planned out...it could not fail of succeeding." Population 100 (*Statistical Account*, vol 16 p.273)

GOLSPIE *Golspie, Suth*
Sutherland
"We are busy laying out a plan for a village, thought of by you when you were last here" - 99 year leases (R. J. Adam *Sutherland Estate Management* (1972) vol ii, p.43 Lady to Lord Stafford 17 Jul 1805). "At last here is the Golspy plan - the houses to be built in the terms I mentioned" (ibid, p.48 7 Aug 1805). Plans drawn up by David Wilson (Sutherland Factors Accounts and Vouchers 1807/14)
Plan - no date, no author (Sutherland Papers)

GORDONSBURGH or FORT WILLIAM *Kilmallie, Inv*
Gordon
One of the three settlements established under the Act "Anent the Bigging" of 1597. Village layout remodelled by John Baxter (GD44/28/34 Tod to Ross 8 Dec 1776) to include a square (GD44/51/16 Campbell and Cameron to Tod 26 May 1794)

HELMSDALE *Loth, Suth*
Sutherland
Initial plans (1810) blocked by tenurial problems, not resolved until 1816 (R. J. Adam *Sutherland Estate Management* (1972) vol i, p.xxv). "Enclosed you have a plan of the intended town of Helmsdale. It is laid out exactly from [William] Forbes plan and the lines of the streets have been well considered. They are not run entirely at right angles both for the look and to suit the lie of the ground with the approach from the road. Dunrobin St and Mound St we think may do for curing houses" (Stafford CRO, D593/K/1//5 Loch to Suther 25 Dec 1817). See J. Loch *Improvements* (1820) pp.126-128 for account of fishery buildings.
Plan - [William Forbes] "Commenced building 1814" (Loch Improvements (1820) pl.4)

INNESTOWN *Lochalsh, Ross*
Hugh Innes of Lochalsh
"On the bay of Auchterryre". Leases advertised in the *Inverness Journal* 10 Sept 1813

ISLE ORNSAY or CAMBUSCROSS *Sleat, Inv*
Macdonald of Sleat
Suggested as site (GD221/98 Diary 15 Jun-12 July 1799). "The plans for a village at Oransay or Island Diarmot may lay over for considera- tion . . . the orders relative to village already issued to the chamberlain will afford sufficient work for a considerable time." (GD221/16/98 Murray to Dick 24 Apr 1800). "I saw Mr Elder from Camuscross here last week and he stated that as Lord Macdonald and his commissioners did not build a village . . . within the three year limit in his agreement . . . he would not give up Elandiarmid" (GD221/53/35 Campbell to Campbell 10 May 1802). Only seven lots let "till the situation of the village is determined on" (GD221/53/39 Campbell to Campbell 1 July 1802)

JEANTOWN LOCHCARRON *Lochcarron, Ross*
Mackenzie of Applecross
"Jeantown yields at present triple the rent it did some years ago, when the site was part of a farm" (G. S. Mackenzie *Ross and Cromarty* (1813) p.248)

KINGUSSIE *Kingussie, Inv*
Gordon

"Repaid to James Robertson W.S. the expense of advertising the new village of Kingussie in the Edinburgh and Aberdeen newspapers - £6-19-0 . . . paid Mr Hog's and Mr Tod's expenses in August 1799 on their journey to Badenoch to lay out and feu off said village - £21-7-4" (GD4451/7/28 Factors Accounts). In fact, Kingussie had long before been canvassed as a village site, notably in George Brown's survey of Badenoch: "In the event of a village or new town being erected in Badenoch the haughs of Kingussie would be the most proper place, and the most central in the country. It is well watered for the accommodation of bleachfields and manufacturers of any kind, and easy access from the kings high road" (SRO CR8/195 Survey of the Parish of Alvie p.29). For a detailed account of the foundation of Kingussie, see the first rate series of articles in the *Strathspey and Badenoch Herald*, 18 Jun 1971 - 17 Dec 1971 by G. A. Dixon.

KYLEAKIN *Strath, Inv*
Macdonald of Sleat
Proposed as village site in 1799 by John Blackadder in his survey of the Macdonald Estates (SRO RH2/8/24 p.35). "1812 - Feby 18 McKinnon McKenzie & Co. Expenses of an Entertainment laying the foundation of the village of Kyleakin" - £59-7-2; Jan 1813 account for workmen "cutting and lining the Front Street" and "measuring the streets and laying the Back Street" (GD221/49 "James Fergusons Account" 2 July 1818). The village plan was a comprehensive failure: "It may be easily imagined that few persons of capital or respectability could think of building in so remote a place as Kyleakin either for business or pleasure and therefore the plan and style of building proposed by Mr. Gillespie though in itself very neat and well conceived, is at present totally inapplicable to the situation. Everything must have a beginning and it cannot be reasonably supposed that in the present age at least, an Isle of Skye town should start at once into splendid existence" (GD221/117 Report on Macdonald Estate, 1830 N. Maclean p.105)
Plan - J. Gillespie 1811 (RHP5998/31,32; other copies in Sutherland and Hamilton archives)

LAIRG *Lairg, Suth*
Sutherland
William Young enthusiastic about the idea of a village at Lairg (R. J. Adam *Sutherland Estate Management* (1972) vol ii, pp.142-143 Young to Marchioness of Stafford 17 Apr 1811)

LETTOCH *Abernethy, Inv*

Grant of Grant
"If Mr [George] Brown or a surveyor from him goes up . . . the intended village above Lettoch may be all lined out" (GD248/1544 Grant to Grant 18 May 1798)

LEWISTON and NEW LEWISTON *Urquhart, Inv*
Grant of Grant
An interesting example of one village supplanting another within 30 years of the latter's foundation by the same proprietor. The relocation of the village was occasioned, at least in part, by the desire of Grant to move the settlement out of the view of his house at Balmicaan (GD248/1549 Grant to Beaton 19 Nov 1805). Village based on the linen industry to ·be established (GD248/49/3/1 Shaw to Grant 26 Jan 1767). Plan drawn up by Alexander Taylor (GD248/ 242 "Memoir as to the intended village at Kilmore Octr 1769"). Account for cutting the lines of the village 3 Jan 1770 (GD248/ 42/6/1 Accts William Falconer). 30 houses built, but of "a very temporary kind" and not to the original plan, "which was to have some cross streets, and an area for a market .place". William Cumming therefore suggests regularisation and draws up a new plan for the village (GD248/713/8/50 "Notes and explanations relative to the survey of Lewistown taken in May 1801" William Cumming 3 Jun 1801; GD248/1028 Factory Account, Urquhart 1801-1802). Inhabitants of old village to move into new one (GD248/1549 Grant to Beaton 11 Nov 1805)

LOCHBAY *Duirinish, Inv*
British Fisheries Society
Plan drawn up in October 1789 by James Chapman, apprentice to George Brown (GD9/3 p.448). Report and new plans drawn up by Thomas Telford in Jun 1790 (GD9/3 pp.577-580). Full details of the settlement are to be found in J. Dunlop *British Fisheries Society* (1978)
Plans - Thomas Telford 1790 (GD9/3 p.580) and 1791 (RHP 11791)

LOCHBOISDALE *South Uist, Inv*
Clanranald (possibly for the British Fisheries Society)
Lease of land at Lochboisdale reserving the right to Clanranald "to dispose of as much of the lands hereby let as shall be sufficient for building the towns and villages presently proposed for the encouragement of the fisheries" (GD201/2/55 Tack of Hugh Macdonald of Torburn 6 Sept 1786)

LOCHINVER *Assynt, Suth*
Sutherland
Recommended as vilage site by William Young in his report on Assynt, 1811 (R. J. Adam *Sutherland Estate Management* (1972) vol i, p.127). Payment to John J. Roy, land surveyor, Sept 1811 for "laying out the village of Loch Inver and for drawing sketches of the same" (Sutherland Factors Accounts (Vouchers) 1811-12). 12 feus set by 1812 (R. J. Adam vol ii, p.167)

LOCHMADDY *North Uist, Inv*
Macdonald of Sleat
Reference to the "late establishment" of a village there (GD221/13/30 "Memo for Lord Macdonald" 1796). Payment to George Brown "for a survey and plan of an intended village at Lochmaddy made in 1798" (GD221/124 Factors Accounts 1798-1799). "I will send my plan of the village grounds at Lochmaddy . . . I made a few remarks on the foot of Mr Cumming's report which you will find rolled up with the plan" (GD221/37 Robert Reid to Campbell 1 Mar 1800). The reference to "Mr Cumming's report" suggests that the 1798 plan may have actually been drawn up not by George Brown himself, but by his apprentice, William Cumming.

LOCH SKIPPORT *South Uist, Inv*
Clanranald
"Last July [1789] Clanranald applied to the [British Fisheries] Society through Mr [George] Dempster for leave to withdraw his offer of Loch Skipport, which was agreed to - He has since begun a village there as his private undertaking; and a number of settlers have come in" (GD9/3 "Matters for Consideration laid before the Directors" 9 Feb 1790 p.449). Reference to "certain grounds at Loch Skipport formerly intended as a village" in the Clanranald Trustees' Minutes of 17 Mar 1799 (GD201/5/1233/31 p.34) would suggest the plan had been abandoned by this date.

LYNCHAT *Alvie, Inv*
Macpherson of Balavil
(New Statistical Account p.983)

PITTENDRAIL *Rogart, Suth*
Sutherland
"I have fixed on a beautiful situation for a village at Pittendrail" (R. J. Adam *Sutherland Estate Management* (1972) vol ii, pp.142-143 Young to Marchioness of Stafford 17 Apr 1811). Payment for "lotting

off feus" 1 May 1812 (Sutherland Factors Accounts 1812-13/12)
Plan - George Alexander May 1811 including cottage design
(Sutherland Papers)

PLOCKTON *Lochalsh, Ross*
Mackenzie of Seaforth/Hugh Innes of Lochalsh
"I shall be under the necessity of employing D[avid] Urquhart the
surveyor to lay out the villages of Plock and Dornie" (GD46/17/3
Fairbairn (Seaforth's secretary) to Seaforth 1 Mar 1794). "Mr Innes
[the new proprietor of Lochalsh] had a surveyor, a Mr [William]
Cumming with him" (GD46/17/19 "Report to Lord Seaforth" Apr
1801). This, given the date of Cumming's plan of the village, would
suggest that Cumming was drawing up his plans of Plockton at the
time. Plockton made a Burgh of Barony (SRO SIG2/55 Hugh Innes
of Lochalsh, 1808). Feus in village advertised in *Inverness Journal*
30 Sept 1808 (see also advertisements in the same newspaper 31
Aug 1810, 8 Mar 1811 and 10 Sept 1813)
Plan - Printed plan by William Cumming 1801 (National Trust for
Scotland, Balmacara)

POOLEWE *Gairloch, Ross*
Mackenzie of Gairloch
99 year leases for building lots advertised; "the proprietor will give
every possible encouragement to the establishing and carrying
on of any manufactory for woollen cloth" (*Inverness Journal* 20 May
1808)

PORT GOWER *Loth, Suth*
Sutherland
Port Gower "promises to become a large place. At one meeting I
have set no less than 24 feus (house and garden ground) to the
natives all of whom are to build neat cottages; small farmers, fishers,
shoemakers, tailors and weavers, and I have laid out ground for
houses to 14 fishermen who I have no fear of getting from Buchan
when the buildings are ready for their reception, and I have written
to Simpson the Midgarty tenant who is now in Banff to ride east to
Peterhead to purchase tiles for the houses and to go through all the
fishing villages to see about the men as it will be of the utmost
consequence to get two industrious crews to settle in Port Gower.
With proper example I think all the villagers will at last take to the
sea and whoever lives twenty years will see all the eastern shores
filled with an industrial seafaring population." (R. J. *Adam
Sutherland Estate Management* (1972) vol ii, p.162 Young to

Marchioness of Stafford 19 Feb 1812) "Paid Alexander Stronach's expenses with a crew of fishermen at Buchie anent settling at Port Gower 20 May [1812]" (Surtherland Factors Accounts 1812-1813/ 12). Port Gower was unusual among planned villages in so far as the proprietor bore the cost of the erection of 14 pantiled seamen's cottages (Sutherland Factors Accounts 1813/3 and 6). In 1817, in a further and, in the short term at least, successful attempt to encourage the inhabitants by outside example, Dutch fishermen were settled in the village, being provided housing at a peppercorn rent (D593/ K/1/3/5 Suther to Loch 30 Aug 1817; D593/K/1/5/7 Loch to Suther 13 Jan 1818; D593/2/2 "Report on the English and Scottish Estates" Sept 1818 p.117)

PORTREE *Portree, Inv*
Macdonald of Sleat

"I have employed [Matthew] Stobie this last week in looking at Portree and planning a future village in that place" - "I have planned a complete city at this place . . . the present plan consists only of two and twenty houses with one acre of ground for a garden behind each of them; and a large space behind the gardens which is divided into inclosures of about eleven acres; all the gardens and inclosures are of a rich fine soil and the place where the houses are to stand is a rocky poor spot, quite level and very well calculated for the purpose. I am so full of the scheme that I fancy I see the street and the shops and warehouses on every side . . . though my plan is so far confined within very narrow bounds, it is capable of being extended much farther" (MS1309 ff.249,254,255 James Macdonald to Mackenzie 15 Oct 1763 and 23 Oct 1763). James Macdonald's brother states his intention to carry on the work begun at Portree (GD221/ 11/28 Macdonald to Secretary of Board of Forfeited Estates 6 Mar 1781). Feus to be granted (GD221/13/30 "Memo for Lord Macdonald" 1796). Villages lots "all taken" (GD221/53/39 Campbell to Campbell 1 July 1802)

SHIELDAIG *Applecross, Ross*

Said to have been built c1810 by a company formed to provide trained seamen for the Navy (*Parliamentary Papers: Reports from Commissioners on . . . Highland Crofters* vol xxxv, 1884, pp.1896-1897)

STORNOWAY *Stornoway, Ross*
Mackenzie of Seaforth

Originally established under the 1597 Act, Stornoway gained feu extensions at Goathill in 1792 (David Urquhart, surveyor) and Inailet in 1794 (GD46/1/544 "Inventory of Map and Plans"; GD46/17/3 Fairbairn to Seaforth 20 Feb 1794; GD46/17/13 Fairbairn to Seaforth 16 Apr 1795 and "Peter Fairbairns Intromissions" 1 Nov 1795)

UIG *Snizort, Inv*
Macdonald of Sleat
Regulations drawn up (GD221/15/1 "Extracts from the Standing regulations of such as relate to villages" 29 Apr 1802). "12 cots taken, two given up" (GD221/53/39 Campbell to Campbell 1 July 1802)

ULLAPOOL *Lochbroom, Ross*
Annexed Estates Commissioners/British Fisheries Society
The Commissioners *coloniae* settlement of 1756 (I. Adams *Peter May* (1979) *passim*) was superseded by the Society's major village, founded on the same site in 1788. Full details are to be found in J. Dunlop *British Fisheries Society* (1978). The initial layout was the responsibility of David Aitken (GD9/3 p.151). Further plans were put forward by Thomas Telford in 1790, but these were not implemented (GD9/32/1 Letterbook of Thomas Telford p.39-46 1 Nov 1790, pp.49-53 3 Jan 1791)
Plans - [Peter May, 1756] (RHP 3400)

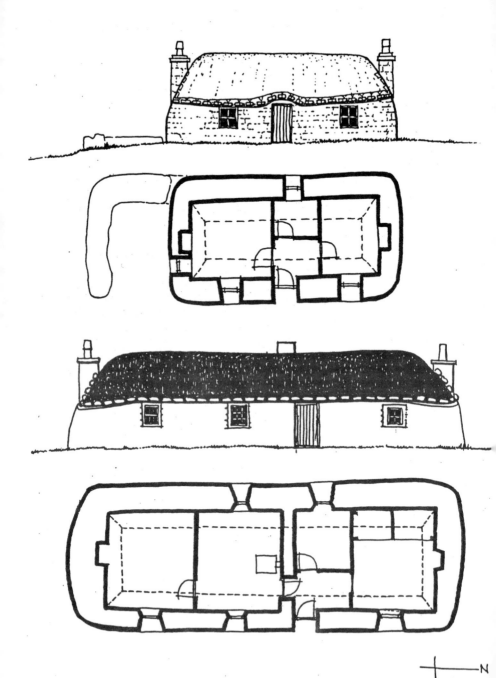

N

Above: "Hostel", Claddach Baleshare, N.Uist. Below: Sidinish, N.Uist.

Bruce Walker
TRADITIONAL DWELLINGS OF THE UISTS

The traditional dwellings of the Uists have many unique features
which are in imminent danger of disappearing. The rate of
destruction is alarming and has been accelerating steadily over the
last fifteen years, particularly since Britain entered the European
Economic Community and EEC grants became available to the local
authority. The situation has now reached the critical point where
it is difficult to comprehend the sequence of development of
building types in any individual township, even over the last
hundred years. In the more obviously traditional townships some
of the stages in the development of the Uist house have been
completely eradicated, whilst in others the complete sequence of
evolution has been lost including the thatched croft houses of the
1880s and later, along with their corrugated-iron, mass-concrete,
timber and masonry replacements. All that remains are: the ruins of
some thatched houses; the shells of some 1930s masonry houses,
renovated to be almost unrecognisable; and a series of anonymous
modern bungalows. This is largely the result of local authority
pressure, stemming partly from the availability of EEC grants and
partly from a growing conviction amongst the populace that all
evidence of the past should be swept away since it has been all
to often the subject of ridicule and patronising comment from
outside observers who invariably fail to comprehend the significance of that which they are castigating.

The plea that a complete sequence of traditional dwellings be
recorded in detail, or better still be preserved intact or allowed
to change at a more natural pace, is not simply a romantic notion
that part of the past be fossilised. It comes from a firmly held belief
that many of the principles behind the organisation and construction
of traditional dwellings are still viable and only require to be better
understood and imaginatively reinterpreted to make a significant
contribution to contemporary housing. The application of some
of these principles in contemporary housing projects can be
compared with the reintroduction of old bloodlines into modern
livestock to change the characteristics of the animals to meet the
demands of both consumer and farmer.

It was with this conviction in mind that the author approached
various grant-awarding bodies for support. The Architects

Registration Council for the United Kingdom (ARCUK) awarded a grant for the study of traditional dwellings in each of four townships. The townships chosen were: Borve, Berneray, Harris; Locheport, North Uist; Howmore, South Uist; and Smerclate, South Uist. Unfortunately three years elapsed between the identification of the townships to be studied and the award of a grant by ARCUK. During this period three of these townships were largely redeveloped and the type of survey originally envisaged was no longer possible. In its place it was decided to survey the last of the thatched houses in each of these settlements, but even this presented problems. At Locheport only one such house remained, and that in a semi-ruinous condition. To broaden the survey in this area it was decided to survey the last remaining thatched house in each of the two adjoining settlements of Claddach Baleshare and Sidinish. Unfortunately, although these survivals illustrate the individual characteristics of the building techniques used by each of these townships, they can not be taken as being truly representative since the sample is too limited.

The detailed surveys were carried out by two survey teams each covering the buildings of two townships. The first team comprised Dallas Mechan, Christopher Paterson, Annette Ratcliffe and Brian Watts. The second team comprised Peter Bell, Bruce Clark, Jonathan Jones and Andrew Smith. All had completed the BSc course in architecture at Duncan of Jordanstone College of Art, Dundee and one years' practical training in an architect's office. Dallas Mechan had left architecture and had completed the museums course at the University of Leicester and is now Assistant Curator at Kirkcaldy Museum and Art Gallery. She directed Team One whilst the author acted as co-ordinator and directed Team Two. An independent photographic survey was carried out in advance of the main survey by Michael Walker of the Dundee Photographic Workshop. Dr Jonathan Bell and Mervyn Watson of the Ulster Folk and Transport Museum studied the farming methods and agricultural calendar which illustrated the time available for the building or repair of houses. Roger Leitch made sound recordings of various crofters who had either built or had repaired their own houses and a young artist, Derek Robertson, sketched the various informants during the sound recording interviews. The ARCUK grant covered most of the out-of-pocket expenses but all personnel involved gave their time and expertise gratis.

HISTORICAL BACKGROUND

The history of housing on the Hebrides is somewhat confused. On superficial examination it appears that the subject is well documented and fully understood but when the evidence is examined in detail it becomes apparent that most of the published material is based on the work of Captain F.L.W. Thomas RN[1] even although he recognised his own work on the subject to be: "drawn from a limited area, for even of this group of islands but a small portion came within my observation: much remains to be done in the way of excavating, planning and measuring"[2]. Unfortunately this advice remained unheeded and Captain Thomas remains the principal source on this class of dwelling.

The remainder of the published material gives the impression of being contradictory. This stems partly from the date of recording, partly from the areas visited, and partly from confusion as to the class of building being described, be it the home of a laird, tacksman, farmer, crofter, cottar or squatter.

The Thatched Houses of the Old Highlands[3] is often taken as an authoritative source and the author, Colin Sinclair claims to be able to classify the thatched houses of the Highlands in three simple categories: Hebridean, where the hipped roof sits on the inner face of the wall and the wallhead is left exposed on the outer side; Skye, where the hipped roof covers the wallhead; and Dalriadic, a form of gabled house similar to early improved farmhouses and cottages of eastern and central Scotland. He infers that these dwelling types are indigenous to the three areas: the Outer Hebrides; the Inner Hebrides; and the Western Highlands. In this respect he criticises Boswell for describing a Hebridean type of house and claiming that these were frequently found on Skye[4]. On consulting other more reliable sources, it is obvious that Boswell was correct and that this class of house was still known on Skye in 1948 when Åke Campbell, a Swedish ethnographer from Uppsala University, surveyed one of the last complete examples. This house had only been abandoned the previous year[5]. Other reliable sources, that should have been consulted by Sinclair, show that, at the beginning of this century, this class of house was still to be found on mainland Scotland but that the distribution pattern was gradually shrinking towards the Western Isles[6]. Trying to establish the original distribution is even more difficult as most eighteenth and nineteenth century descriptions are somewhat ambiguous since most of the reporters were not building experts but simply interested observers. In this respect the descriptions are non technical and even when the reporters use technical terms they may well be misinterpreting the meaning of the term. In this respect there is nothing to preclude the terms "black-house", "creel-house" and "turf-house" applying to the same building in certain circumstances whilst applying to quite different structures in other descriptions. The fact that dramatic changes took place in the housing stock of the western districts of Scotland in the second half of the nineteenth century is borne out by statements made by the principal recorders of these buildings and by the photographic evidence. Thomas states: "that the houses of the west of Lewis although representing a very old style, are yet of comparatively recent erection"[7]. This statement can be supported by a study of the changes that can be observed in a series of photographs taken in any particular Highland district over a hundred year period. Where the sequence is particularly complete and well documented it is interesting to note that when changes do occur, they appear to happen very quickly, for example, the adoption of the use of nets over the thatch rather than continuous roping[8].

It is also apparent that Sinclair's classification is far from adequate to deal with the wealth of building types and constructional techniques to be found in the buildings of the west coast of Scotland and that even taking the roof types that formed the basis of Sinclair's classification, there are many variations entirely unaccounted for. He completely fails to see that each of the roof types in his classification can cover buildings of the same plan form and he completely ignores the innumerable variations in plan form and hearth position; the changes from byre-dwelling to dwelling house; changes in building materials, constructional techniques and types of roof structure, adapted to the needs of individual communities. Unfortunately much of this information is now lost forever, but some hints can be gleaned from the surviving descriptions, visual evidence and the few surviving structures.

Bearing these limitations in mind, it is worth re-considering the available evidence to provide some historical background to the buildings surveyed in the four townships of Borve, Berneray; Locheport; Howmore and Smerclate.

The housing situation in the Western Isles is quite different from other areas of Scotland. This is due to special circumstances arising partly from the poor economic situation existing there, a situation solved in part by the breaking up of improved farms to provide crofting settlements. In building terms this resulted in traditional houses being demolished to clear the original settlements; improved farmhouses and steadings being erected on the new farms; and the eventual subdivision of these improved farm buildings and the erection of new croft houses in the new crofting settlements.

The pre-improvement situation on the Hebrides is described by Johnson in 1773.

"The habitations of men in the Hebrides may be distinguished into huts and houses. By a *house*, I mean a building with one storey over another; by a *hut*, a dwelling with only one floor. The Laird, who formerly lived in a castle, now lives in a house; sometimes sufficiently neat, but seldom very spacious or splendid...

Huts are of many graduations; from murky dens, to commodious dwellings. The wall of a common hut is always built without mortar, by a skilful adaption of loose stones. Sometimes perhaps a double wall of stones is raised, and the intermediate space filled with earth. The air is thus completely excluded. Some walls are, I think, formed of turfs, held together by a wattle, or texture of twigs. Of the meanest huts, the first room is lighted by the entrance, and the second by the smoke-hole. The fire is usually made in the middle. But there are huts, or dwellings of only one storey, inhabited by gentlemen, which have walls cemented with mortar, glass windows, and boarded floors. Of these all have chimneys, and some chimneys have grates.

The house and the furniture are not always nicely suited. We were driven once, by missing a passage, to the hut of a gentleman, where, after a very liberal supper, I was conducted to my chamber, I found an elegant bed of Indian Cotton, spread with fine sheets. The accommodation was flattering: I undressed myself, and felt my feet in the mire. The bed stood on the bare earth, which a long course of rain had softened to a puddle . . .

The petty tenants, and labouring peasants, live in miserable cabins, which afford them little more than shelter from the storms."[9]

Captain Thomas confirms the existence of a wide range of building types in parts of Lewis, St Kilda and the Applecross peninsula[10]. The 1885 Royal Commission on the Housing of the Working Classes extends the distribution of black houses to include the Outer Hebrides, Inner Hebrides, Sutherland, Ross-shire and Inverness-shire[11]. They also attempt to define the term "black-house" as follows:

"The black-houses are all of a simple and rude character differing, however, materially from each other. There are houses...in which the entrance is common to the cattle and to the human inhabitants, and in which there is no partition between the byre, the kitchen, and the sleeping apartment: in which all the inhabitants, human and bestial, live under the same roof in the same open space. There are other houses in which there is a common door but in which there is a partition between the cattle and the human inhabitants. There are some in which there is no window in the wall but a window in the roof. There are some houses in which there is a fireplace in the centre of the floor, but with no proper chimney. And there are other houses in which there is a chimney, or more than one chimney, in the wall. There are some houses in which, perhaps there is no window at all, and in which light is admitted entirely by the door or the aperture through which the smoke escapes . . . Some . . . might be termed unfit for human habitation . . . others . . . are by no means uncomfortable . . ."[12]

Earl Brownlow, one of the commissioners asked the following questions.

"The questions that I wish to ask you are entirely confined to black houses. I think the definition of a "black house" is a house that is built entirely without mortar, is it not? - Yes.

And many of them have no chimneys? - Many of them have no chimneys.

And in many cases I believe the cow lives in the house? - In some cases but not all. These customs are very often local. In one place you have one custom, and in another you find a different kind of house, and the byre with a separate door.

Are black houses built as much now as they were a few years ago, or are they going out? - They are going out.

- I understand the black house is always built by the tenant.

Do you find that the people who are living in black houses are anxious for better houses or are they satisfied with the black house as it stands? - I am afraid that they are too well satisfied with the houses as they are.

. . . . I have heard that their great objection to going into other houses is their being cold.

. . . . It is not a rule that they have a cow in the house except in Lewis."[13]

Turning to the other side of the country, the Commissioners asked about the situation in the county of Angus.

"Are any of the old black-cottages left? None, we never had any of them in my recollection in the lower part of Forfarshire. We had turf cottages in the upper parts.

In the glens? - In the glens; what we call divot cottages, made of sods or divots."[14]

The reporter in this instance saw nothing to connect the "black-house" of the western districts of Scotland to the "divot-cottages" of the Angus glens, but the question remains - what was the basic difference between these two building types? It cannot be the difference between byre-dwellings and dwelling house since byre-dwellings must have existed in Angus as that time since the occasional example was still to be found as late as the 1950s[15]. By this time these buildings had become stores but the low partition between cattle and humans allowed the beasts to look directly into the kitchen. It cannot be the difference in building materials since Joseph Mitchell describes the Lewis black-house as being:

"Built of turf and thatched with straw or heather, huddled together very irregularly, and generally in villages, the grass growing frequently on the tops of the walls and the roofs. There are no windows; a hole admits the light. The door is low, generally from four to five feet. The house is from thirty to sixty feet long; the greater part appropriated by the cattle, and the family part separated occasionally by a mere turf partition.

We examined two of these houses. The walls were of rough turf; and some common boards put together for two or three beds, with one or two cribs on the floor, apparently for the children.   An old woman lay in some decayed hay in a bed. The fire was in the centre, over which hung the pot, and the children were sitting on the floor around, while two or three large stones appeared to serve as seats for the adults. This part of the hut was hung round with fish, pieces of rope, net, or other   implements   used either in fishing or agriculture."[16]

The existence of a link between the dwellings of the eastern and western districts of Scotland is not as far-fetched as some writers would have us believe. Sir Kenneth Mackenzie giving evidence to the 1885 Royal Commission stated:

"I was myself exceedingly surprised a short time ago, in talking to an old man of 90 years of age close to where I live on the east coast, where the houses are now all decent habitations, to be told by him that in his father's house, in the beginning of the century, there was no division between the cattle and   the people, and that was universal at that time. He attributed the improvement to the women; when an improvement began he said that the womenkind emulated one another in improving the houses and cleaning and decorating them . . ."[17]

To return to the Western Isles. The Rules and Regulations for the Lewis Estate in 1879 give considerable scope to the   tenants as regards their choice of materials and   constructional technique, yet at the same time they appear to be describing the type of house that Sinclair calls a Skye type. The only difference between the two types of building is that the Lewis Estate does not demand that the byre be a separate building. The Estate Rules read:

"The dwelling houses be erected by the tenants . . . shall be of stone and lime, or of stone and clay pinned and harled with lime, or with stone on the outer face, and turf and sod on the inside, and roofed with slates, tiles, or straw, or heather with divots . . . each house to have at least two apartments, with a glazed window in the wall of each, and a closet or small room, with chimneys in the gables, or other opening for smoke in the roof; the thatch or covering not to be stripped off or removed for manure; the byre to be built at the end or the back of the dwelling house, as the site may admit, and to have a separate entrance. In the byre a gutter to be formed for manure, which shall be regularly removed to the dung heap outside."[18]

Sinclair's Skye type of house does not appear to have been particularly commonplace on Skye at that time. John MacPherson, a crofter and fisherman in Skye gave the following evidence to the Commission:

"The houses generally are similar to one another . . . The houses are mostly all in three divisions; generally the cattle in one end, and the kitchen in the middle, and the whole of the people at the other end in one room. They are about thirty six feet generally in length, and almost thirteen feet or fourteen feet broad. The walls are about four feet or five feet high.

They have a sloping roof, have they not? - Yes, a couple of trees. There is nothing in the wall but earth between the stones, no lime, and earth below their feet; there is no wood below their feet or above their heads.

You see the rushes of the roof from the room? - Yes, it is straw that we used to have; but the quantity of land is so scarce that it will not feed their cattle and thatch their houses; and they are leaky . . .

Are the beasts in the same room with the people? - No, there is a partition between them, or something of that sort.

Is the partition carried up the whole height? - Yes, or half-way up; not, it might be, to the top.

Is there a separate entrance? - No, sometimes, it is the same door in most of them.

There is not a slated house on the estate that I am on belonging to a crofter, except two tradesmen's and the lairds dog-house; it is slated.

What are the worst houses like? - There is no worst amongst them, they are not kept so well at Elgoll and Sconser . . .

Are the people satisfied with the condition of their houses? - No, they are not . . .

The whole family sleep in the room, however many there are . . .

There is no other place for them, unless it will not hold them, and then they will have a bed in the barn, if they have a barn.

I thought you said that houses had been built in Scalpa for £10. - In Skeabost.

Those houses are some think similar to the kind that I told you of, that one built with earth; there is no lime or anything about. They are black-houses? - Yes."[19]

The Reverend Angus McIver gives some idea of the number of buildings in this class in Lewis:

". . . over 3,000 crofters and 1,000 cottars living in houses of one or two rooms, in most cases one room . . . built by the people themselves . . . and kept in repair by the people themselves . . roof of straw . . . secured with heather striggs . . . no ceiling in some cases; in most cases it is otherwise . . . great accumulation of cattle dung . . . clear it out once a year . . . when they remove this dunghill there is apt to be fever."[20]

Another description of a crofters house in Lewis reads:

"The walls are built of stones gathered from the fields, and fitted roughly together. To keep out the wind they are made five feet thick, and both side walls and gable ends are but six feet in height. On the inner edge of these massive walls the roof timbers rest. They are covered with thatch, a foot or two thick, there being no well-defined ridge, but a rounded top like an elongated beehive. The houses vary from thirty to sixty feet in length and are fifteen feet wide. You stoop your head as you enter by the only door, and if your visit is in July, you make an unexpected descent of a foot down to the earthen floor. If your visit is in March the inside level is higher than the surface of the ground, for you step upon a thick mass of wet cattle-bedding and dung, which has accumulated since the previous summer. Coming in from the light of day you stumble in the deep obscurity, which is barely relieved by the single window of a foot square. You make your way over the spongy surface, and at length find yourself on firm ground as you approach the large peat fire burning on the middle of the floor, the smoke from which fills the whole house, and finds a partial egress through the thatch for there is no chimney. You receive a hospitable welcome from the host, who courteously invites you take a seat. Overhead the cackling of the hens, which are striving for the warmest roost near the fire, attracts your notice. Near the window there is a deal table, and dimly visible through the smoke are two pallet beds at the inner end of the apartment. The lowing of a calf at the far end of the house, beyond the door by which you enter, leads you to grope your way thither, and you are told that at present the rest of the bestial are grazing outside.

In this house, such as it is, the crofter has secured the two essential requisites of dryness and warmth. The walls and thatch effectually keep out the wind and the rain. None of the heat is lost, arising from the generous fire, round which a large circle can gather. His roof, and the floor of the cattle end of the house, furnish a valuable supply of manure for the potato fields. In spring the men and women clear out the whole accumulation of cow dung and bedding, which they carry in creels, and deposit on the field. Later in the summer they strip from the roof the thatch which is now thoroughly saturated with the soot of a twelve-month's fires, and spread it as a top-dressing to the potato-drills, where it proves an invaluable stimulant.

These houses are now happily becoming the exception rather than the rule. Most of the larger houses have a partial division between the cow end and the central kitchen apartment, beyond which again there is a second partition, dividing off the inner room which has a fire place, with a chimney in the gable, and another window. In this room may be found a table with a cloth spread, and chairs to sit on, but the temperature is perceptibly lower, as so much of the heat escapes. The suggestion has been made by Canadian emigrants, who have revisited their old homes, that instead of the open-fire-place in the wall, the Canadian plan should be adopted of a stove in the centre apartment, from which the flue could be carried into the inner room, and thence into the cow-house, built at the back of the dwelling. This would provide a clean and tidy heating apparatus, which would diffuse as much warmth as was required both for the family, the cattle, and the poultry. Every now and again the flue could be swept out, and the soot kept by itself for the potato field."[21]

It must be borne in mind that the housing being described above was occupied by crofters and that there were many superior buildings occupied by farmers, tackmen, tradesmen, merchants and lairds. At the other end of the social scale, the Royal Commission stresses that:

" . . . there would still remain a class of habitations in the Highlands and Islands, and especially in the Islands . . . impossible to deal with, and that is, the . . . squatter, inhabiting a house built against an estate regulation, built in defiance of the orders and the will of the proprietor, a habitation perhaps made of a few sticks and turf, without even stones - for such exist. If eviction were tried people would be worse off still."[22]

The situation in 1885 is summarised as follows:

"The condition of the dwellings of the crofter and cottar populations of Scotland differs very materially, and they may be divided into three classes: 1st, the black houses of the old and of the improved type, 2nd, the white houses, and 3rd, the houses of a superior kind constructed in recent years.

Black houses are common to Skye, the Long Island, and the Western Islands, where they are found in great variety; they may also be seen on the northern and western coasts of the mainland, and to some extent in the central Highlands, but are said to be generally disappearing. Some of them are considered fairly comfortable, but the majority are undoubtedly confined, dark, miserable, and unhealthy. They are built by the crofters themselves, without skilled labour and without imported materials. They differ very considerably in condition, according probably to the means and tastes of the occupier, the worst being found in some parts of Skye and the Island of Lewis. Some of them, for instance, have only one entrance for the cattle and the inhabitants, and have no partition between the byre, the kitchen, and the sleeping apartment, all the inhabitants human and animal being under the same roof in the same undivided space. Many of these houses have no windows at all, light being admitted only by the door or the aperture through which the smoke escapes, the fire being usually of peat burned on a flat stone in the centre of the house. The accumulation in these dwellings of the dung of the cattle and other unwholesome substances, the prevalence of dirt, the absence of separate rooms and of fresh air render the inhabitants of them very liable to the contagious fevers which from time to time break out in the crofter villages, chiefly in the spring and this type of house may be said to be the worst that exists, though very common among the crofter population . .

There are other black houses in which there is only one door, but which contain a partition between the cattle and the human inhabitants. These houses, though of a rude character, are frequently free from drafts, and not uncomfortable, or so unfit for human dwellings as the old black houses. These may be called the improved black houses, and are the work of co-operation, more or less, between the tenant and landlord, the tenant bearing the greater portion of both labour and cost.

People . . . are said to be unusually healthy, long lived, and some of the most moral of Your Majesty's subjects. Doubtless this is in spite of the condition of their homes, with which they are not, as a rule, dissatisfied.

The white houses are found also in the Western Highlands and

Islands, but they are not peculiar to one locality, though they are most common on the eastern side of the country, and in Orkney and Shetland. They differ from the black houses, being built partly with skilled labour, and with materials imported from other districts. In appearance they resemble a common description of cottage in the Lowlands, though the materials are more perishable, and the roof more defective in material. They have chimneys in the gables, and windows; the walls are built with mortar; the floors are made with boards, earth or flags; the partitions and ceilings are of wood and clay roughly put together; the roofing is of boards covered with thatch, or felt and tar, and occasionally slated . . ."

". . . poorest class of sub-tenants and squatters . . . the worst type is to be found amongst the crowds of squatters in parts of Lewis who construct mere hovels, made perhaps of a few sticks and turf, without stones, and built in defiance of the estate rules, and against the orders and will of the proprietor . . ."[23]

The situation had improved somewhat by 1917 when the Royal Commission on the Housing of the Industrial population of Scotland Urban and Rural published its report. This was similar in its findings to that of the 1885 Commission but the numbers of black-houses had decreased and those of improved houses had increased. They also added a new category to the "Old" and "New" black-house categories described by the earlier Commission. The additional category was known as the "Renovated black house", and was described in the following terms:

"A renovated black house usually contains three apartments separated with wood-lined partitions. The kitchen is open to the roof and the floor is of earth. The old walls may be retained, but are usually reduced in width, flushed with lime mortar on both faces and window openings inserted: and end gables or stone chimneys. The thatch is put on in the usual way, but the roof rests on the outer edge of the side walls, and the stones attached to the roof ropes hang clear on the wall face. These houses, as a rule, are very comfortable, and not so draughty as the black house; and damp although still prevalent, is not so pronounced. The cost of these alterations is from £20 to £25 in cash, according to size and finish."[24]

Although the situation had improved considerably, other contemporary reports show that:

". . . In many hundreds, perhaps thousands, of the black-houses, the cows are housed practically with the people, entering often by the same door. This is technically known as "cattle-housing" . . . it is still extremely common (on Lewis)."[25]

The range of building materials in use was still extensive and

Mackenzie writes:

". . . lay aside for the moment those rigid ideas about stone and lime, or bricks and mortar, or wood and iron, or stones and peat, or stones and sand, or even about caves in the rock. All of these types of houses are, in Scotland at least, found to be occupied by human beings."[26]

SUMMARY OF THE FINDINGS OF THE SURVEY

The drawn survey confirmed that there is a range of hitherto unrecorded dwelling types in the Uists which fall between the Lewis blackhouse and the Skye crofthouse as described by Colin Sinclair in 1956.

The croft houses on the island of Berneray dated from after 1900 when the island was resettled. They are built to two basic plan types: one with an internal masonry gable containing the flue for the kitchen fire and having four rooms: the other, a three room plan of similar type to an improved farm cottage. The four room type is normally asymmetrical in external expression; the three room type can be either symmetrical or asymmetrical. Both types have thick walls comprising two skins of masonry with a rubble fill. The walls are battered externally and occasionally internally. They are low, seldom exceeding 1.85 metres high and the wallheads are partly exposed round the entire perimeter of the dwelling. The window openings are not lintelled across the entire width of the wall but only in the recess under the roof. Some of the houses are surrounded by a cobbled pavement and a narrow drainage ditch. Externally, the ends of the houses take three forms. Normally they are either apsidal or roughly squared with swept corners but very occasionally they are squared. These features are often associated with the supposed age of the dwelling - the older the house the more rounded the ends of the building but in Berneray all thre types can be found in a single group of dwellings known to have been constructed at approximately the same time. This probably reflects the resettling of Baile and Borve with people having different building traditions. The thatched roofs are all crudely hipped, not with pean rafters but with a rough lean-to arrangement against the outer trusses. The thatch is applied in soft rounded forms without the use of special ridge treatments. The principal thatching material is "bent" or marram grass cut from the sand dunes of the Atlantic coast. This is held in place with either fishing net or wire netting, weighted with stones attached to the netting at eaves level. This is achieved by inserting a rope through

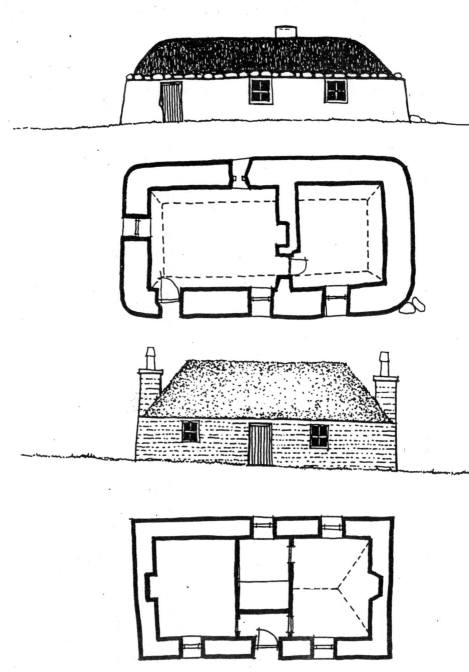

Above: Locheport, N.Uist. Below: Howbeg, S.Uist.

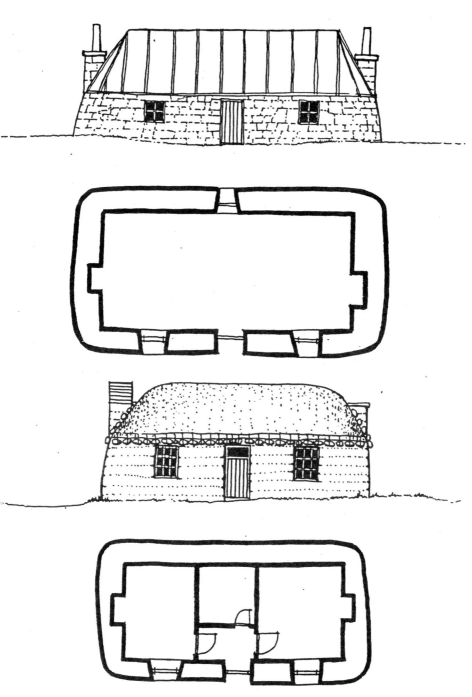

Above: Mr Collier, Smerclate, S.Uist. Below: 8 Howmore, S.Uist.

the bottom strands of the netting, leaving loops at regular intervals into which the stones are inserted, then twisted round to tighten the rope. This makes it easy to remove and replace the stones thus allowing the netting to be lifted for thatch maintenance or renewal. The thatch is laid over an undercloak of turves supported on ropes and thatching battens. On reaching the lowest thatching batten the rope is passed under the batten, carried round the outside of a short rafter then back under the batten before passing back over the roof. The short rafters spanning from the wallhead to the bottom thatching batten are usually made up from barrel staves or short pieces of driftwood. The fireplaces in the end walls of the bedrooms are served by tower chimneys built off the wallheads. The outer face of the chimney is set back from the wall face leaving a slight scarcement. Internally the walls are strapped, lathed and plastered or matchboarded. Ceilings are normally about 2.20 metres high with a slight coombe to the wallhead. The internal partitions comprise a series of studs with nogging formed of small pieces of broken stone set in clay mortar. Above this the gablet is formed of a series of vertical poles set into the top rail of the stud partition and attached to the sloping members of a roof truss at the top. Heather ropes are then woven back and forward, wattle fashion, between the uprights to form a mat which is finished with a top dressing of clay. One of the most interesting buildings on Berneray is the byre at 19 Borve. Although termed the byre only one end of this structure was used to house cattle and the building is probably the last survival on the island of a byre dwelling. It certainly fits some of the nineteenth century descriptions as regards layout and size. It also has a window at the end away from the byre gutter. This is an unusual feature in a byre, normally reserved for the most superior of model farms in the east-central Lowlands. Most Scottish farms light the byre with rooflights as provided at the byre end of this building. The roof structure is also much less regular than those described previously and uses irregular pieces of driftwood and old barrel staves to form the support for the turf undercloak. This is very different from the regularly roped structures described above. The other byre surveyed by Cawthorne had a similar roof structure to that at 19 Borve.

The croft houses of North Uist are similar in form and construction to those described on Berneray but they do have some independent features. The only one common to all the buildings surveyed was the method of fixing the rope rafters. Here the rafter rope is tied to the bottom thatching batten by a second rope which is wound round the batten, the spacing being sufficient to fix two ropes on each full turn. The house at Claddach Baleshare owned by Mrs. Tosh and now used as a youth hostel is of the three roomed type and almost identical to its counterparts on Berneray. It is reputedly the oldest house in this North Uist group and is the only thatched house in the area where the wallheads project round the entire perimeter of the house. It was recently re-thatched by Mr. Tosh using bent taken from the sand dunes.

Although Claddach Baleshare is quite close to Locheport and Sidinish it lies close to the machair on grass covered ground whereas the Locheport and Sidinish houses are on the shore of a sea loch penetrating the heather clad moors of eastern Uist. They utilise this heather as a thatching material providing what is considered to be a much heavier but more durable roof. The thatch finishes flush with the outer face of the wall on each of the long elevations but the wallheads project at the ends of the buildings and round the sweep of the corners. The wallheads tend to drop towards the corners creating a very organic form. The walls are also whitewashed externally. These houses are of the central gable type described in Berneray but at Sidinish the older style of furnishing survived, at least in part. The north bedroom had two built-in curtained beds along the west wall. The room to the south of this, at the west side of the entrance passageway, had contained the loom but was latterly used as a small unheated bedroom. The kitchen had a cast-iron stove projecting from the internal gable. To the west side of this was a long settle made from re-worked driftwood which had been attacked by marine borers prior to its removal from the sea. The tunnels had been filled with putty and the whole settle painted. The roof over the south end of the house had collapsed burying the dresser on the south wall of the kitchen and the furnishings of the bedroom beyond. This roof collapse gave a perfect opportunity to record the roof construction in detail even to the various layers of thatch which had been applied. It is interesting to note that one of these layers was of straw and another of bracken but that the remainder of the thickness was made up with layers of heather. The Locheport croft-house had a similar central gable but only two rooms. The house was entered directly into the kitchen, the room being beyond the central gable. The house was occupied until 1986 but half of the roof has already collapsed, showing the weakness of these structures after the fire is extinguished.

The croft houses of South Uist are very different in design and construction to those of North Uist and Berneray. Basically they are built to the plan form adopted for small Lowland farmhouses, croft houses and cottar houses but with an external aesthetic more akin to the Hebrides. They are superficially symmetrical in plan and elevation with a central door leading into a short passageway with the kitchen to one side and the room to the other. A small room at the back of the passageway was traditionally entered off the kitchen but some have been altered to give direct access. This mid room is unheated and the other rooms have end wall fireplaces served by tower chimneys built off the wallhead. The roofs are thatched with bent over turf and the thatch finished flush with the outer face of the wall round the entire perimeter of the house and is netted and weighted as described previously. The thatch generally has a rounder form, thickening up in the mid span of the rafters. The main difference between these houses and their North Uist counterparts is in the section through the kitchen end of the house. The South Uist kitchen follows the tradition of eighteenth and nineteenth century farmers' halls, from the east-central Lowlands, where the kitchen or hall end of the house was open to the apex of the roof and the other rooms were lofted to provide high level storage space. Some open hall kitchens still survive in Howbeg and South Lochboisdale but the majority of the houses have had ceilings added since the late 1940s.

Surprisingly these ceilings still recognise the old tradition and rather than being inserted just above wallhead level they have a large coombe section tapering up to a small ceiling placed under the collars of the A-framed trusses. The majority of these houses had been built this century, the example at Howbeg, which still retains its open-hall kitchen, dated from circa 1935. One house stood out as being exceptional: the croft house at 8 Howmore was very much higher in the walls, and ceiling, than any of the other buildings in the vicinity. It appears to have been in existence in 1881 when the first edition of the Ordnance Survey was prepared and was occupied by a family of shepherds. Not only is this building higher in the walls, but it has larger windows, a fanlight above the door, ceilings at wallhead level, high quality adze-dressed timber roof trusses, proper purlins and rafters, ceiling joists and is in every respect superior to the other croft houses in the settlement. Donald Maclean, the owner, thinks it was an estate building, built for the estate shepherd or tacksman in the third quarter of the nineteenth century. Mr. Collier's croft house at North Smerclate appeared to have higher quality walls than the other houses in this group and it may be that the tacksman in each settlement had a superior quality house built by estate masons at a date when the rest of the populous were still inhabiting turf walled dwellings.

Many of the inhabitants of the townships on the east side of

South Uist moved to Eriskay when their townships were cleared for a second time in the 1880s. A photographic survey of Eriskay dwellings was organised to try to establish similarities in building forms and techniques. Although this was the intention there were no complete thatched croft houses surviving on Eriskay and the survey failed in that respect. It did however produce some very significant material, particularly the ruins of some turf and alternating stone and turf walled structures in close proximity to formerly thatched croft houses. Usually ruins of this type are little more than low mounds determining the outline of the building but on Eriskay the walls were still standing to approximately a metre high suggesting that these buildings had been roofed at a much later date than normal. These buildings may well have been inhabited in some form until the 1930s or 1940s but local inhabitants were evasive when the subject was mentioned. Another interesting feature was the thatched roofs of some of the older outhouses. These had a peculiar irregularity and when viewed with the light were barely distinguishable from the large rocks which form a prominent feature of the Eriskay landscape.

In so far as proving that the existing forms of thatched house are, on the whole, between sixty and one hundred years old, and in the case of Howbeg only fifty years old, the survey has been a complete success.

This survey is part of a continuing study of Highland housing and as such has made an important contribution to our understanding of the development of housing types in these remote areas. The houses of the Uists, far from illustrating a type of building providing a direct response to an inhospitable climate, as suggested by many previous researchers, confirm the survival of housing types and building techniques known to have existed in east-central Scotland in the eighteenth century but largely abandoned in these areas by the end of the first quarter of the nineteenth century. The surveys have also provided detailed information on various forms of roofing and walling, some of which are known from early descriptions but all hitherto unrecorded by detailed measurement.

The information collected will now be married with information from other studies carried out by a range of disciplines and the results will appear in a series of articles, or in a monograph on the subject.

NOTES AND REFERENCES

1   F.L.W. Thomas "On the primitive dwellings and hypogea of the Outer Hebrides" *Proceedings of the Society of Antiquaries of Scotland* vol 7 (1866-68) pp. 153-196

2   Ibid.

3   Colin Sinclair *The Thatched Houses of the Old Highlands* (1953)

4   Ibid.

5   Åke Campbell Mss Survey (1948)

6   C4409.1 "Appendix and Index as to Scotland" *Royal Commission on the Housing of the Working Classes. V Minutes of Evidence* (1885)

7   F.L.W. Thomas *op.cit.*

8   Photographs taken by George Washington Wilson towards the end of the nineteenth century show a distinctly different style of thatch and building to those taken early this century.

9   Samuel Johnson *Journey to the Western Islands of Scotland in 1773* (1927) pp. 91-93

10   F.L.W. Thomas *op.cit.*

11   C4409.1 *op.cit.*

12   Ibid. p.104

13   Ibid. p.97

14   Ibid. p.97

15   Bruce Walker *The Agricultural Buildings of Greater Strathmore 1770-1920* Ms PhD Thesis University of Dundee (1983)

16   Joseph Mitchell *Reminiscences of My Life in the Highlands* vol 1 (1883 reprint 1971) pp.232-233

17   C4409.1 *op.cit.* p.107

18   Ibid. p.95

19   Ibid. pp.114-117

20   Ibid. p.117

21   Ibid.

22   Ibid. p.106

23   C4409 *Second Report on Her Majesty's Commissioners for Inquiring into the Housing of the Working Classes: Scotland* (1885) pp.9-10

24   C8731 *Royal Commission on the Housing of the Industrial Population of Scotland: Urban and Rural* (1917)

25   Ibid. p.428

26   W. Leslie MacKenzie *Scottish Mothers and Children* (1917) p.165

27   Buce Walker "Lofted Open-Hall Farmhouses in Scotland" *Vernacular Building* 13 (1988) pp.45-49

Hugh Cheape
HORIZONTAL GRAIN MILLS IN LEWIS

Grain mills of the horizontal type that have often been described in the relevant literature as "Norse Mills" or "Danish Mills" are a prominent and significant element in Scotland's relict material culture. Although evidence for them appears to be scant and fragmentary, research has shown that at least latterly they were most common in the Northern Isles and in Lewis, the areas of apparently densest Norse settlement. Assumptions were made by scholars of earlier generations that these mills were a strong indication of the extent of the Norse cultural province and a significant survival of it[1]. Gaelic, in this respect, provided a firmer indicator of type and origin in that the so-called Norse mill-type was consistently referred to as *muileann beag, muileann dubh* or *muileann làir* or variants of these terms. Where Gaelic has declined or has gone out of formal use, Gaelic speakers will tend customarily to adopt the term "Norse Mill" from English because it appears to be the prevailing term as both description and explanation of origin[2]. Unfortunately they will generally turn their back on the more significant inference to be drawn from their own Gaelic in favour of the mistaken precept of English.

It is significant that when the authors of the parish surveys in the *Statistical Account* made reference to horizontal mills in the eighteenth and nineteenth centuries, they would use terms such as "Highland mill" or alternatively "black mill", itself the direct translation of *muileann dubh*[3]. Traditional learning had no such illusions about Scandinavian origins as the antiquaries of the nineteenth century; indeed the Gaelic learned classes attributed little more to *na Lochlannaich* than godlessness, a penchant for covetousness with brutality, and a general nuisance-value. Geoffrey Keating writing in his beautifully clear and idiomatic form of literary Gaelic, common to both Scotland and Ireland in the seventeenth century, recounted the tradition that the legendary Cormac MacAirt, King of Ireland, had seen fit to send to Scotland for joiners to make him a mill[4]. There may be no more significance in this than the indication of the strong and well-established *Kulturgebeit* of the *Gaidhealtachd* and of the exchange of learning that was a firmly entrenched tradition until the cultural links between the two countries were severed in the seventeenth century.

Horizontal mills which harnessed water power to drive an ungeared mechanism for grinding grain represent a form of early technology whose cultural province extends far beyond the *Gaidhealtachd* of Scotland and Ireland. They certainly did not originate in the north Atlantic area, as earlier scholars had suggested. Although speculation over a locatable origin or polygenesis are entirely beyond the scope of this study, we should at least be aware of the widespread adoption of horizontal water wheel mill technology in Europe, in Asia and beyond.

We are now clear that the "Norse" and "Danish" mills are not a representative feature as such of Scandinavian material culture or its influence, or of the north Atlantic maritime province. Research has not yet in fact produced a proper distribution map of this element of material culture either of continental or of world status. Nor are facts about this technology widely known such as its persistence in many areas, in spite of the consistent reference to it as a "primitive" mill-type, into the twentieth century. Thus Lewis shared this element of material culture with regions such as North East European Russia, the Caucasus, Turkey, Yugoslavia, Romania and France, as well as with the more obvious Norway, Sweden and Faroe[5]. Even in many of these areas, technical advances were known and adopted but a distinction might be maintained such as, for example, that a vertical water wheel was used for pumping water only.

Technical advances, especially in those areas less well endowed with a sufficient supply of water, confined themselves to increasing the potential of the motive power of water rather than increasing power and drive within the mill itself. The *arubah* mill of the Eastern Mediterranean for example, of which there is comparatively plentiful evidence as early as the fourth century A.D., was worked with a sophisticated system of rising water cisterns while still depending for its drive on an ungeared horizontal mill wheel[6].

Earlier linguistic and lexical studies, such as the essays in honour of Dr Ronald Cant published in *The Scottish Tradition* in 1974, have demonstrated patterns of language retreat and advance and consequent interrelationships, and of linguistic data of extraordinary richness and regional variety. Although drawing on a wide range of terms of varying Celtic, Scandinavian and Northern English origin, Dr Alexander Fenton concluded in a detailed study of corn-drying kilns that "it will be some time before Gaelic lexicography can provide research data comparable in linguistic and historical range to that of the Scottish 'period' dictionaries"[7]. By looking at the related topic of mills in which research can uncover a certain amount of data, it can be complementarily demonstrated that Gaelic possesses an extraordinarily rich vocabulary of technical detail in areas of material culture and, more significantly perhaps, that this vocabulary is not recorded or adequately or knowledgeably explained in the standard dictionaries.

The format of dictionaries and the presentation of linguistic data, unless carefully or selectively qualified, can give an impression of universality within a cultural province or *Sprachgebeit*. Thus if we look up mill or *muileann* in Gaelic dictionaries, the relative lack of material may lead the unwary to draw conclusions without taking account of variation of lexical factors over time and space. The latter-day existence of horizontal mills on the north and west coastal fringes of Scotland, for example, may deceive us into assuming that they were restricted to the present-day *Gaidhealtachd.*

When written documents proliferate in the twelfth, thirteenth and fourteenth centuries, the word *Scoticus* or *Scoticanus* was customarily used to distinguish elements of contemporary civilisation that belonged to an older order before the advent of Anglo-Norman speech, culture and institutions. The qualifying *Scoticanus* is most commonly found referring to the country north of the Forth and Clyde and, we may reasonably infer in certain contexts, to the material culture pertaining to Gaelic-speaking Scotland, mainly north of the Forth. Thus, it may be that *molendina Scoticana*, many of which appear to have been on the eastern fringes of the Highlands, were horizontal mills[8]. This is not necessarily or satisfactorily proven and a note of caution in evaluating this sort of evidence is sounded by assumptions emanating from modern fieldwork. Small but entirely ruinous mill buildings in now remote or deserted locations in the Highlands and Islands were not necessarily mills on the horizontal principle. Indistinctly surviving traces of small mills, for example, have been examined in Skeabost, Skye, and in Mingulay, Barra. In both instances what were at first assumed to be horizontal mill sites were clearly "vertical" mills, that is, rectangular buildings erected tangentially to rather than over a water-course or lade and powered by geared shafting from a small, undershot, mill wheel.

Descriptions in depth and detail of horizontal mills while they were still in operation in Scotland and by those who were properly acquainted with them are rare if not unique. One such is the detailed account of the mill in Kirtomy, in the coastal parish of Farr in Sutherland, by Alexander Mackay who belonged to the adjoining crofting township of Swordly[9]. Born in 1829, he in common with so many of his contemporaries left Sutherland about 1855 and settled in Edinburgh where he died in 1916 in his eighty-eighth year. Moving as he did in the city circles of expatriate Highlanders, he realised that he could make a contribution to the considerable cultural (but not political) interest in Gaelic that was typical of Scotland's large cities in the nineteenth century, the reception areas of a displaced, migratory and often desperate population from communities such as his own of *Dùthaich Mhic Aoidh*.

Most significant in Alexander Mackay's account is the comprehensive terminology in Gaelic for all the technical detail of the mill in Kirtomy and, we may assume, of horizontal mills in the northern coastal area, a cultural province in which language, for example, shows distinctive dialect and idiomatic features. The mill, described as it was when in use in the 1830s and 1840s, fell into ruin about 1866 or 1867.

This decline in the fortune of these little factories was common to the whole north and west mainland in the mid nineteenth century and to most of the Hebrides where they had been such a prevalent feature of the economy. By contrast, the horizontal mill survived in active use in the Northern Isles and in Lewis where the traditional economy of crofting and fishing continued to be the livelihood of a more densely settled pattern of population. Hence, it is these latter island areas which yield up most evidence for the enquirer, not necessarily of the material prehistory of the mills, but more prominently of their history as practical and functioning technical adjuncts to the farming and crofting economy.

The evidence for horizontal mills in the relatively more densely populated Island of Lewis is prolific. Evidence in the form of traces on the ground and embedded in place-names shows them to have been widely distributed round the coastal townships of the Island consistently both with long-term and with changing settlement patterns. One estimate put the number conservatively at 150 and a superficial glance at the evidence both documentary and on the ground suggests that each township had four, five and six or more horizontal mills[10]. Many accounts which make reference to them as a clearly important aspect of material culture and integral part of the economic infrastructure tend to content themselves with repeating a limited range of facts and evidence or drawing inferences or generalising from specific examples which may be less relevant than imagined to the historical circumstances of Lewis[11].

Some of the fault for this lies with the standard works of reference. Dictionaries of Gaelic are poor recorders of material culture, tending to focus on the literary, the philosophical or even folklore in vocabulary and idiom. Exceptional in this respect is the dictionary compiled by the eternally enthusiastic Surrey man, Edward Dwelly, whose work was published in fascicules at the turn of the twentieth century. The coverage of material culture varies however, areas such as boats and fishing not surprisingly being relatively fulsome. Water mills (*s.v. muileann*) and hand mills (*s.v. brà*) are also more fully considered than other aspects, including a number of specialised terms obtained from a Donald Murray of Lewis, then living in Aberdeen[12].

The familiar elements of everyday life and material culture were below the regard of the dictionary makers who were ministers or priests and men of the upper strata of society, typically the descendants of the old tacksman class. Yet, if any specific area of material culture is looked at in detail, the potential still exists to uncover a rich and varied vocabulary in which every detail bears its own name and idiomatic identity. Thus fifty or even a hundred years after these mills might have gone out of use, knowledge of the very rich technical vocabulary can still be recovered. The list below has been compiled from a range of sources and, it must be stressed, refers to horizontal mills in Lewis only[13]. Assumptions about the universality of these terms within the *Gaidhealtachd* are unacceptable until proven in individual cases[14].

A'chlach uarach - the upper millstone or top stone.
An t-sùil - the hole or "eye" in the centre of the top stone, approximately 5in diameter.
Cladhan a'ghràin - grooves picked on the under surface of the top stone to move the grain centrifugally between the grinding stones.
An dual - driving bar or "driver" fixed in the eye of the top stone.
Leabaidh an duail - socket for the driving bar, cut as a recess in the underside of the top stone, approximately 1in deep and extending 6in each way.
A'chlach iarach - the lower millstone or nether stone.
Maoladh - when the millstones became smooth and bare, they would be picked with a sharp and hardened hammer newly sharpened by the blacksmith.
A'chiste mhìne - the meal box, approximately 2ft wide and 2ft 6in long, was constructed with upright stone slabs and the joints between the slabs were filled with *riasg* or peat-moss; this boxed-in area, also known as *an t-slochd* or "the pit", contained the meal as it was cast out from between the millstones.
An treabhailt (no drabhailt) - the hopper to hold the grain above the

millstones; this might be variously of willow basketwork, of woven grass (*muran*), of straw rope (*sloman connlaich*), or latterly of wood. In the case of willow, grass or straw rope, the hopper was slung from the rafters or *casan cheangail* with three ropes.

A'bhròg - the shoe, forming a small spout or chute to direct the grain from the narrow base of the hopper into the eye of the top stone. When the *bròg* was not directly above the eye of the millstone, a lump of peat (*caoran monach*) would be twisted into one of the hopper's ropes in order to shorten it and bring one side of the hopper up slightly.

Clagan (no glagan) na bròige - the shaker or clapper which, lying on the top stone and attached loosely to the shoe, agitated the shoe to maintain the flow of grain down from the hopper into the eye of the top stone.

Toll an fheuchainn - hand hole for inspection of caulking or packing for the lower millstone. In the corner of the *slochd* to the side of the stones, the *toll* or hole was located. It was closed off with a *sop* or small bunch of straw. When it was thought that the mill was losing grain seed, the man working the mill would put his arm through the hole to inspect the head of the mill wheel. If there was only mill dust on the head of the wheel, everything was in working order, but if there were particles of grain on the head of the wheel, the stones were not fitting properly or the mill needed adjusting.

Cubadh - tightening the wooden plug that filled the hole in the lower millstone and through which the spindle or *dealgan* turned the top stone; this might be done by putting extra wedges or *geinnean* into the wooden plug.

An tigh-làir - the ground floor or under-house.

Roth a'mhuilinn - the wheel or rotor; the preferred *roth* was made from the base of a boat's mast (*crann bàta*).

Liaghan - blades; it is significant that the Gaelic *liagh* (singular) denotes a large spoon or ladle implying that the end is shaped, concave and scooped out.

Dealgan - spindle; a wrought iron bolt, axle or crank fixed into the top of the *roth* and slotting into the *dual* or "driver" in the top stone and transmitting the drive vertically and directly to it.

Torchan (Torghan) - wrought iron bolt, crank or gudgeon fixed axially into the base of the roth.

An t-sàil aotromachaidh - the lightening beam by which the top stone could be raised or lowered in order to grind rougher or finer as required or as the force of the water allowed.

Geinn - wedge to hold the position of the lightening beam when raising or lowering the top stone.

An t-sàil bhuinn - the horizontal, sole or ledger beam on which the *roth a'mhuilinn* rotated. It was fixed to the foundation wall at one end and connected with the *sàil aotromachaidh* at its outer end so that it could be raised or lowered in order to raise or lower the *roth*.

Sorchan - rest or socket which received the point of the *torchan* or lower spindle of the *roth*.

An t-sàil dhìreach - the upright beam, fixed to the outer end of the horizontal sole beam and extending through the floor of the millstone platform into the upper chamber.

Lunn - bearing plate fixed onto the wooden *sàil bhuinn* or sole beam and receiving the point of the *torchan*. The *lunn* might have a series of recesses into which in turn the *torchan* was fitted when the recess being used allowed the *sàil bhuinn* to be worn right through.

Dàm na muilne - the mill dam built to provide a head of water when required to drive the mill it would generally be closed by a stone dyke with an opening in it.

Slugan na muilne - a deep and narrow channel directing the water into the mill. This is approximately equivalent to the word "lade". The word *slugan* usually denotes "windpipe" or "throat".

Dorus an uisge - the water gate in the wall of the mill through which the wooden channel takes the water from the dam and directs it straight onto the rotor blades or *liaghan an roth*.

An t-amar fiodha - the wooden trough or channel which takes the water from the mill dam; the *amar fiodha* consisted of two parts, *an t-amar beag* or little channel was the part nearest to the *roth a'mhuilinn*, and *an t-amar mór* or large channel the part nearest to the dam. The *amar beag* could be moved up or down and from one side to the other in order to direct the rush of water straight onto the blades of the rotor.

An tuil - the flood of water through the *amar* to be directed against the blades of the rotor and to provide the motive force for driving the mill. The Gaelic word *tuil* is used in a general sense to denote "deluge", "heavy rain", "flood", or "an overflowing of running waters". The Biblical Flood by which God destroyed mankind and all creatures of the earth and sky not taken into Noah's Ark was referred to in Gaelic as *An Tuil Ruadh*.

In concluding this list of terms, it should be emphasized that with few exceptions these words and phrases are not included or are not interpreted in the published dictionaries. Much of the vocabulary of this glossary, including rich, alliterative phrasing in Gaelic, was the inheritance from a corn mill belonging to the township of South Bragar, described significantly as the fourth from Loch Ordais[15]. Without locating the site exactly, this would be approximately at OS Grid Reference NB 284484. The mill stones were of granite or Lewisian gneiss from Beinn Ghuidimul above Dalbeag. The dimensions of the building were recorded; the inside length was 14ft and the width 10ft, and the walls graduated in thickness from 6ft to 4ft. These measurements were qualified by the comment that the size of the mill and of the millstones would depend on the volume of water available.

Beside technical vocabulary, there are further sources which throw light, both subtle and straightforward, on the subject of horizontal mills. We shall consider on the one hand some literary references and on the other, some graphic evidence.

The texts of one or two waulking songs recorded within recent years include the line: "*Muileann air gach sruthan sléibhe*" ("A mill on every mountain stream"), this no doubt being a stock phrase of encomium, the inclusion of which in what might often be extemporary verse was deemed to heighten the effect that it had on its audience[16]. It might seem paradoxical that the building or existence of a mill should be considered fitting subject matter for a list of attributes or achievements of the Gaelic warrior hero or nobleman. There are further examples of the conservatism of oral tradition preserving details of older sets of values by which seemingly mundane elements of material culture appear to be elevated to the status of indicators of noble virtue. A simple, functional, hand-thrown, coarse pottery of local clay, known as *crogain*, that appears to have had a continuous tradition of manufacture in the Hebrides since at least the early Iron Age, supplied such a reference. The ability to turn clay into fine cups was for example added to the stock of conventional phrases of panegyric[17].

It is ironic that these old Gaelic texts were neglected when scholars first began to record the particularly rich oral tradition of Gaelic-speaking communities in the late eighteenth century following the publication of Ossian and in the course of the nineteenth century. The waulking or chorus songs in particular were felt not to be suitable for literary treatment, being popular songs of improvisation with the function of accompanying, enlivening and regulating labour processes. The early scholars were particularly interested for example in the literary folktales or *Märchen*, the long hero tales of international origin and with exotic parallels in other parts of the world such as "The Arabian Nights" or the *Gesta Romanorum*.

Just as the *seanchas* and local historical lore was ignored until almost the turn of the twentieth century, so were the chorus songs, both texts and music, in preference for the poetry and song of ballads, formal encomiastic verse, and the extended prose works typical of early Celtic literature. The chorus songs were sometimes recorded because of the subject matter and social ambience, such as eulogy on a celebrated figure otherwise known to history, rather than necessarily any intrinsic merit. As more works of literature in Gaelic were published in the nineteenth century, each successive publication tended to draw on earlier anthologies with the consequence that awareness of the Gaelic literary corpus was biased away from what had become the commonest elements.

When examining literary references to mills, it should be borne in mind that many of the texts take us back to the Highlands and Islands of the sixteenth and seventeenth centuries. This was an heroic society whose values evoked the still living traditions of *Cù Chulainn* and the *Tàin*, or "Cattle Raid of Cooley", the Iliad of Celtic literature conventionally described as the Ulster Cycle. The main function of prose and verse was to praise famous men; it was a literary vehicle by which to enumerate and describe the qualities of a warrior aristocracy, their actions in battle and in the chase, and their descent from kings and heroes. The audience wished to recall and be taught on the one hand of their undying example of bravery and on the other of their charity and hospitality. References to mills fit into the bardic and poetic convention of describing circumstances of fertility and prosperity, being seen as the consequence of the rule of a good king. By contrast, it was well known that the consequence of the death of rulers was that the land became infertile, animals and even humans became barren and the weather turned wild in sympathy. Mills would then be lying in ruins. The celebrated *Oran na Comhachaig* of more than 80 verses puts mills into the proper Gaelic context of the rule of a noble and virtuous leader. It was composed probably in the late sixteenth century by a *Domhnall mac Fhionnlaigh* who lived in the Keppoch country in the vicinity of Loch Treig. The poem begins with a dialogue between the poet and an aged owl in which the bird is urged to recall everything it has seen and heard. The bird recalls the ancestors of the MacDonnells of Keppoch, in particular Alasdair Carrach, the founder of the house of Keppoch, and his son Aonghus. Apart from referring to Fersit as his place of abode, he singles out the one virtue for reference that he raised a mill on the Lair Burn: ". . . . *'S rinn e muileann air Allt Làire*". As the poet continues by lamenting the chaos of warring and raiding that was plaguing Lochaber at that time, the virtue of mill-buildng is lent some point. Since Alasdair Carrach, the founder of the Keppoch family, was a brother of Donald, Lord of the Isles, and fought at Harlaw (1411) and Inverlochy (1431), his son Aonghus must have flourished in the mid fifteenth century[18].

As folklore and folksong came to be more highly regarded, contemporary with the development of the disciplines of anthropology and ethnology in the late nineteenth century, some other aspects of the history of horizontal mills were laid bare. A single, well-known example of song codifies a great deal about Highland and Hebridean social and economic history. *Am Muileann Dubh*, a song composed and preserved as *port-a-beul* or mouth music, is a form of nonsense verse that has, beyond the poetic function, the social purpose of making good the absence of musical instruments primarily for dancing and secondarily (and more usually today) for straightforward entertainment:

1. *Tha 'm muileann dubh air thurraban*
   The black mill is rocking

   . . .
   And it wants to try to dance.
2. The nest of the grouse is in the black mill

   . . .
   In the black mill in the summer.
3. The cattle are giving birth to their calves

   . . .
   In the black mill in the summer.
4. There are cockles and mussels

   . . .
   In the black mill from summer.
5. There is many a thing that you would never think of

   . . .
   In the black mill in the summer![19]

In common with the kiln and the smiddy, there is an inference in this that the mill was a place exclusively for the male and this supports other aspects of tradition which demonstrate respectively exclusive roles for men and women in their communities. There is also more than a hint that the "black mill" was the home of the illicit still, a euphemism that is contained in other well known *port a beul, Tha bainne aig na caoraich uile*, known also as "The ewie wi the crookit horn"!

Nineteenth and twentieth century anthologies of Gaelic poetry are scattered plentifully with songs about grain mills. It is significant that there is a consistent note of sadness for times past in most of these modern songs although careful scrutiny may uncover other themes. The example from Bragar, Lewis, translated below, *'Se fàth mo mhulad mar chaidh a'mhuilinn*, uses the township mill as the indication of how the old community spirit of communal reliance and mutual help and support has been destroyed by the pressure of social and economic change in the late nineteenth century:

1. The reason for my sadness is how the mill has become derelict,
   And that I shall not get for baking what I need,
   Although I am wet through from dawn to dusk,
   There is no one now who can understand its workings.
2. The spindle and the axle are rusted into the driving bar,
   Everything about it is upside down,
   The mildewed stones have a melancholy appearance,
   And the elements pouring down on them each day.
3. When the arguments begin their subject will be
   That you should be paying more,
   I possess half a croft and I shall not be so foolish
   As to pay for the grain that you have in it.
4. You thought that you could grind what you pleased
   Without paying a single sixpenny piece,
   But now you will pay before you grind your food,
   What is required to put blades of larch into [the mill wheel].
   . . .
7. The days of kindness have certainly vanished
   And we shall not grind grain in it this year,
   Without ready money the mouth of every sack will be closed
   As was done by Pharaoh's Governor
   . . . [20]

The note of bitterness and sadness behind this and other songs of the same period and mill theme remains largely unexplored. Village poetry, some of it mediocre but some of it sparkling with brilliance and originality, has been something of a closed book to the historian because of the language divide between Gaelic and English[21]. The angers and frustrations of an increasingly desperate population were largely reserved politely for the ears of the communities in which most were still in the late nineteenth century monoglot Gaelic speakers. The Battle of the Braes and the Crofters' War came as a rude surprise to a largely complacent

Pitt Rivers' sketches in his fieldwork Notebooks of the "Norse mill" near Barvas, showing plans, sections and measurements (PRO, Ancient Monuments Inspectorate, Works 39/9). The internal dimensions (upper right) were 18' x 10'7", the doorway 3' wide, the diameter of the millstone 3', the centre of the eye of the millstone 5' from the side wall and 8' from the end wall. The height of the gable of the mill to the ridge was 8'4" and the side wall was 5' high. The hopper which he describes as being made of grass (upper left) was 1'10" in diameter and 2' deep. The millstone platform was raised 1'6" above the floor of the mill, helping to accommodate the "underhouse" and water wheel. The "underhouse" (bottom left) was 5'6" across at its widest point and 4'2" high to the lower surface of the flagstone platform supporting the millstones. The water wheel had 11 blades each about 1' deep and 1'3" long. The sole tree was 5'6" long, the lightening tree 4' long, the upright lightening beam about 4'4" long (bottom right). The entry for the water was 1'2" across and the exit 2' across.

105

106

North Mill near Barrow
Plan of [...] mill stone

104

104

[it has wooden vertical turning wheel below stone]

thickness of top stone 8 inches under stone
[...]

903

103

difference
of wheels
2...0

2...0

2...0

2...0

W. S. Tomkin's drawing of the interior of a "Norse mill near Barvas, Isle of Lewis, August 13th 1885", in his sketchbook in the papers of the Ancient Monuments Inspectorate (PRO, Works 39/6). He shows the hopper made of woven grass and hanging by three straw ropes from the roof couples, and the shoe or spout and shaker or "clapper" for directing the grain from the hopper into the eye of the mill stone

Establishment. At the same time as the Napier Commission enquiring into the conditions of crofters in the Highlands and Islands was in session, other visitors were beginning to come to islands such as Lewis as steam navigation and improved communications opened up the Hebrides to the curious. Between 1883 and 1885, Britain's first Inspector of Ancient Monuments made the most detailed of his tours of scheduled sites of prehistoric significance including those in Lewis. He in common with many of his fellow archaeologists found much to interest him in the Island.

The first Inspector of Ancient Monuments was Lieutenant General A H L F Pitt Rivers. The post was created by the Ancient Monuments Protection Act of 1882, and held by Pitt Rivers from 1 January 1883 until his death in 1900[22]. His first years of office were active, primarily in making tours of inspection, details of which have survived in a series of field notebooks and sketchbooks with pencil entries made either by Pitt Rivers himself or by an assistant during visits to monuments. In one of his notebooks, he made detailed notes and measurements of a horizontal grain mill at Loch Urraghag on the road from Barvas to Carloway, situated approximately at OS Grid Reference NB 324487. His assistant, W S Tomkin, drew the interior of the mill in a separate sketchbook[23].

In the 1860s, Pitt Rivers began to examine his own work in the light of the findings of Britain's greatest naturalist, Charles Darwin, who, in *The Origin of Species* in 1859, crystallised a still nebulous theory of evolution. Pitt Rivers saw himself at the centre of the far-reaching contemporary debate on evolution and progress and formulated his own theories in lectures such as his "Evolution of Culture". He believed that material culture was an integral part of culture as a whole and a vital facet on the understanding of man as a cultural being. He stressed the role of technologies in the evolution of culture, in that culture would tend to develop in pace with the solutions devised for problems as they arose. This did not necessarily find favour with a diffusionist school of thought which described cultures as entities migrating and spreading; in this intellectual atmosphere, the study of material culture was later to become isolated.

Among his strongly held precepts, one in particular still has a strong appeal. Pitt Rivers always returned both in his lectures and in his published work to the contention that material culture could play an important and largely unrealised role in reconstructing the histories of remote peoples and in explaining the evolution and distribution of cultures. He described how material culture should take its place as legitimate evidence in a range of disciplines such as archaeology, history, geography language and linguistics. The words of a contemporary in describing horizontal mills in Lewis and in Shetland reflect precisely the same scholarly attitude towards the concept of "civilisation", its differing rates of evolution and survival, and the inferences to be drawn from certain elements of material culture:

". . . that there may be two ways of looking at rude and primitive practices or objects; and that these ways do not lead us to like conclusions, when we attempt to use such practices and objects as aids in studying the condition of early man."[24]

With the discipline of anthroplogy then in a nascent stage, material culture was beginning to be assessed and given equal weighting in a context which included oral information and observed behavioural data. However soundly based these concepts were, interest in them declined at the close of the nineteenth century and the relatively original thinking and theories of men such as Pitt Rivers languished. Modern scholarship can only regret the opportunities missed by the consequent neglect of fieldwork in relict or sub-recent communities in the Hebrides for example[25]. Scholarly attention focused instead on areas such as art styles, social organisation and languages, and, in addition, disciplines such as anthropology moved away from the museums and into the universities.

This complex fashion and shift of emphasis can be seen in the failure in Scotland of the initiative of scholars such as Dr (later Sir) Arthur Mitchell, quoted above, in the second half of the nineteenth century to create in the National Museums ethnological collections of comparative material to demonstrate patterns of evolution and distribution in the development of civilisation. In formulating his thesis of the survival of the past in the present, Mitchell looked *inter alia* at hand mills and horizontal mills as visible markers and prime examples of a partially prehistoric material culture whose relatively simple technology was appropriate to the economic status of their user communities. In describing horizontal mills in Lewis and in Shetland, Mitchell emphasized the important distinction of status between horizontal and vertical mills, that the former was usually the property of a township or a combination of townships while the latter was the property of an individual giving rise to the system of thirlage which bound the tenant to the proprietor's mill and the exaction of multures or scales of fees in kind. The former was the expediency adopted by persons fully aware of more advanced technologies since "the mill, as they make it, does all the little they want it to do, in the way which best combines economy with efficiency"[26].

The avoidance of thirlage or the heavy burden of thirlage as a feudal exaction was mentioned by several sympathetic commentators. Rev David Mackay, the minister of Reay, for example, described how there were few mills in the Highland area of his parish compared with the Lowland, and how "Highland mills" were maintained in the townships to avoid the burdens of thirlage including the obligation to repair the mill fabric and lade and also to bring in the new millstones[27]. In the lengthy and in many respects outstanding account of his large Hebridean parish, the minister, Rev John MacLeod, described how there was no "public mill" in the whole of Harris though the principal tacksmen have small mills "of a simple construction"[28]. There must remain an element of ambiguity in this phrase whose interpretation depends partly on an understanding of the social and economic status of the principal tacksmen in this context. The balance of evidence favours these being horizontal mills. He continued by describing the common expediency adopted by the sub-tenants to use querns in the absence of mills to grind their corn. This is a note echoed by many of the Hebridean parish accounts.

The number of satirical and uncomplimentary stories and songs in Gaelic against millers is sufficient testimony to their unpopularity and their invidious position in the community, a tradition that can be seen to be co-extensive with mill technology[29]. A single local Lewis story will suffice to exemplify the motif. Kenneth MacKenzie, known as *Coinneach Bàn*, according to one account a man of nearly 7ft tall, was the Tacksman of Laxay in the parish of Lochs and owned the only mill in the area. He increased the fees for grinding the tenants' corn to such an extent that they refused to use his mill. They did their grinding with the *bràth* or quern. *Coinneach* retaliated by requisitioning all the upper stones of the querns in his locality and he dumped them in the estuary of the Laxay River, at a place known to tradition as *Slochd nam Bràth*[30].

REFERENCES

1   Arthur Mitchell *The Past in the Present: What is Civilisation?* (1880); Gilbert Goudie "On the Horizontal Water Mills of Shetland" *Proceedings of the Society of Antiquaries of Scotland* Vol 20 (1885-1886) p.257-297, and see especially pp.290 and 294-297; I. F. Grant *Highland Folk Ways* (1961) p.116; cf E. C. Curwen "The Problem of Early Water-mills" *Antiquity* Vol 18 (1944) pp.130-146, in which the

author puts forward provisional conclusions on their spread in western Europe. Where the terms were common in local parlance as in the Northern Isles, it may indicate a casual and traditional ascription of any element whose origin is mysterious or unknown to the Nordic occupation.

2   See for example John M. MacLeod, "Our Island Heritage. Projects by Leurbost School" *Stornoway Gazette* 6 July 1968.

3   See for example Rev David Mackay "The Parish of Reay" *Statistical Account* Vol 7 (1793) p.576; Rev Archibald MacArthur "The Parish of Kilninian" *Statistical Account* Vol 14 (1795) p149; Rev Robert Finlayson "The Parish of Lochs" *New Statistical Account* Vol 14 (1845) p164.

4   Quoted by Rev Alexander Stewart (ed.) *The Scottish Gael* Inverness [n.d.] Vol 2 p.104.

5   Detailed descriptions and diagrams of horizontal mills in France were published in Bernard Bélidor *Architecture hydraulique; ou l'art de conduire, d'élever et de ménager les eaux pour les différens besoins de la vie* 4 Volumes (1737-53)

6   Shmuel Avitsu *Water Power in Eretz Israel and Abroad* (1969) I-IX

7   Alexander Fenton "Lexicography and Historical Interpretation" in G. W. S. Barrow (ed.) *The Scottish Tradition. Essays in honour of Ronald Gordon Cant* (1974) p.247

8   See for example G. W. S. Barrow *The Anglo-Norman Era in Scottish History* (1980) pp.161-162

9   Alexander Mackay "The Horizontal Mill at Kirtomy, Farr, Sutherlandshire" *The Celtic Magazine* Vol 11 (1886) pp.470-474; Alexander Mackay "The Old Kiln and the Mill" *The Celtic Monthly* Vol 13 (1905) pp.118-120

10   E. C. Curwen "The Hebrides; a Cultural Backwater" *Antiquity* Vol 12 (1938) p.284; Donald Macdonald *The Tolsta Townships* (1984) p.148.

11   See for example Gilbert Goudie "On the Horizontal Water Mills of Shetland" *op.cit.* p.279; E. C. Curwen "The Problem of Early Water-mills" *ut supra* p.141

12   Edward Dwelly *The Illustrated Gaelic-English Dictionary*, Glasgow 5th Edition (1949) p.677

13   National Library of Scotland MS14956 f5-11; Hugh Cheape *Kirtomy Mill and Kiln* Scottish Vernacular Buildings Working Group (1984) pp.33-34; Scottish Ethnological Archive, National Museums of Scotland, MS Archive 1978/102.

14.   See for example E. C. Curwen "The Problem of Early Water-mills" *ut supra* p.141

15   For example: *An taigh-làir, ionad an roth, nan amar, agus an uisge na thuil choprach, thormach agus an roth 'na ghille-mirein a'cur nan car cho luath 's nach fhaicte ach lasadh loinnireach nan liagh. Bha an t-sàil bhuinn fodha.* [The under-house, around the water wheel, the channels, and the water in a foaming white, noisy flood, and the wheel like a whirligig spinning round so fast that nothing was to be seen except the gleaming flash of the blades. The sole beam was submerged.]

16   J. L. Campbell *Hebridean Folksongs* (1969) pp.136,146

17   Hugh Cheape "Food and Liquid Containers in the Hebrides: A Window on the Iron Age" in Alexander Fenton and Janken Myrdal (ed.) *Food and Drink and Travelling Accessories. Essays in Honour of Gosta Berg* (1988) pp.17-18

18   William J. Watson *Bardachd Ghàidhlig*, 3rd Edition (1959) p.250

19   Dr Keith Norman MacDonald *Puirt-a-Beul* (1901) p.15

20   National Library of Scotland MS14956 f7. The writer of this article wishes to acknowledge with gratitude the help and advice given by Donald Macdonald MA, FEIS, FRSGS, in translating this poem into English.

21   See for example Iain N. MacLeoid *Bardachd Leòdhais* (1916) pp.3-4

22   M. W. Thompson "The First Inspector of Ancient Monuments in the Field" *Journal of the British Archaeological Association,* 3rd Series Vol 23 (1960) pp.103-124.

23   Public Record Office, Ancient Monuments Inspectorate, Works 39/6 and 39/9

24   Arthur Mitchell *op.cit.* p.43

25   See for example Hugh Cheape, "Crogans and Barvas Ware Pottery in the Islands" *Stornoway Gazette* 22 January 1983, drawing attention to a series of questions of archaeological and historical relevance for which answers could have been provided by appropriate fieldwork around the turn of the century.

26   Arthur Mitchell *op.cit* pp.42-43

27   Rev David Mackay "The Parish of Reay" *op.cit.* p.576

28   Rev John MacLeod "The Parish of Harris" *Statistical Account* Vol 10 (1792) p.356

29   See for example "Fionn" [Henry Whyte], *Leabhar na Cèilidh* (1898) pp.157-164. The story, *Am Muilleir Cam agus am Balbhan* [The Deceitful Miller and the Dumb Man] is a good example of the relatively poorly recorded humourous tale in the tradition of the international popular tale.

30   John M. MacLeod "Our Island Heritage" *op.cit.*

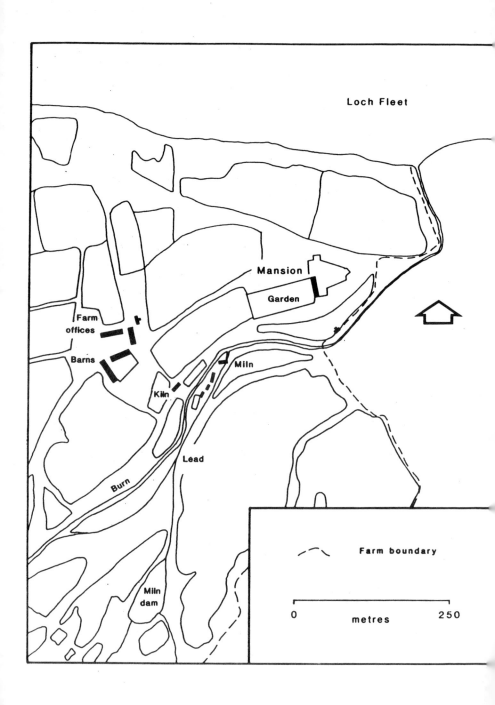

Loch Fleet

Mansion

Garden

Farm
offices

Barns

Miln

Kiln

Lead

Burn

Miln
dam

Farm boundary

0   metres   250

Malcolm Bangor-Jones

ACCOUNTS OF BUILDING WORK AT SKELBO
1723-1787

The "mansion" house of Skelbo in south-east Sutherland is a
building of great architectural significance in the Northern
Highlands. The records which are presented here relate to
building work carried out to the house, farm buildings and girnal of
Skelbo during the period that the Skelbo estate was under
sequestration and will, it is hoped, contribute to the history of this
site[1]. As Geoffrey Stell has written[2], building accounts for this period
in the Highlands are few and far between and the records of Skelbo
are thus of great interest for the information they contain on
building costs, the sources for materials, constructional techniques
and the availability of skilled craftsmen. The records also throw
light on the administration of a sequestrated estate for although
bankrupt estates were relatively common, little has been published
on their management. The seemingly simple process of ranking
creditors and bringing an estate to a judicial sale could, in some
instances, take a considerable number of years. Although there
were regulations surrounding the administration of sequestrated
estates - expenditure on reparations, for instance, had to be
sanctioned by the Court of Session - this does not mean that positive
management was impossible. After all, if a fair price was to be
obtained for a property, then the land had to be kept tenanted and
the buildings in good repair.

In the medieval period the lands of Skelbo belonged to the De
Moravia family, who became the Morays of Culbin. Skelbo later
passed by marriage to the Kinnairds and then in 1529 William
Sutherland of Duffus bought Skelbo from John Kinnaird of that Ilk.
The Sutherlands of Duffus were descended from Nicholas
Sutherland, the second son of Kenneth, fourth Earl of Sutherland.
Nicholas Sutherland had been granted the lands of Torboll in
Sutherland in 1360 and acquired part of Duffus in Moray by
marriage. Alexander Sutherland was created Lord Duffus by
Charles II in 1650 or 1651. However, James, who succeeded as the
second Lord Duffus in 1674, ran into financial difficulties which were
only made worse when he murdered one of his creditors in 1688.
A considerable proportion of the estate in Sutherland was wadsetted

out and eventually the outlying lands of the estate in upper Strathnaver were sold in 1700. There does not, however, appear to be any evidence to support the assertion that Lord Duffus was forced to sell the estate to his second son James, an advocate.

Efforts were made to save the estate. Kenneth, who succeeded as Lord Duffus in 1705, became a naval captain and a scheme, involving Kenneth's younger brother, William Sutherland of Roscommon, was put into operation to buy up the debts affecting the estate. These measures were insufficient and the creditors began to take steps to seize the estate. It was this, perhaps, which prompted Kenneth to take part in the Jacobite Rebellion in 1715. The estate was forfeited and placed in the hands of the Commissioners responsible for disposing of the forfeited estates in Scotland. Skelbo, however, was claimed by John, Earl of Sutherland on the basis of the Act for encouraging loyal superiors of 1715, usually known as the Clan Act. The Earl entered into possession of Skelbo in 1716 and in 1719 was awarded the estate by the Court of Session, under burden of a proportion of the debts. These were considerable and the creditors were able to have the estate sequestrated in 1723. In the meantime, the lands of Duffus had been obtained by Archibald Dunbar of Thunderton.

Although some legal progress was achieved, proceedings were allowed to lapse and it was not until the late 1730's that another attempt was made to bring the estate to a sale. This time the main mover was the Earl of Sutherland who in 1738 had acquired right to some of the principal debts affecting the estate. Unfortunately the earldom itself was heavily encumbered by debt and there was little to spare for fighting lawsuits. Consequently there was no procedure from 1754 to 1765. In 1768 the Court of Session decerned that the Countess of Sutherland must either pay all of the debts affecting the estate or bring the estate to a judicial sale. The Countess and her tutors chose the latter course but experienced considerable difficulties in redeeming the various wadsets on the estate, a task only completed in 1775, and it was not until 1787 that the estate was finally sold.

It is not surprising that during the 64 years of the sequestration the administration of the estate passed through the hands of a number of judicial factors appointed by the Court of Session. The first factor was Sir James Calder of Muirton, a Morayshire merchant and suspected Jacobite who had been greatly involved in the

Sutherland salmon fishings. A sub-factor, William Sutherland of Thomskill, carried out much of the day-to-day administration. Calder was apparently succeeded in 1735 by Eric Sutherland, eldest son of the attainted Lord Duffus and, after his father's death in c.1734, generally known by the courtesy title of Lord Duffus. His factorship was terminated by the appointment of Robert MacAllester in 1738. MacAllester had been a factor for the Earl of Sutherland since 1729 and his appointment thus marks the beginning of the Sutherland family's dominant influence in the sequestration. In 1739 MacAllester appointed Kenneth Sutherland of Meikle Torboll, a wadsetter on the estate and who had taken over as factor the east coast parishes on the Sutherland estate, as his sub-factor. MacAllester was replaced by James MacLean of Capernoch, a local merchant and tacksman farmer, whose factorship lasted from 1743 to 1756. From 1756 to 1787 the judicial factor for Skelbo was Dugald Gilchrist, a former "servant" to the Earl and a factor on the Sutherland estate from 1741 to 1770[3].

Prior to the Rebellion the house of Skelbo was occupied by William Sutherland of Roscommon, who been given a general factory in 1709. Once the Earl of Sutherland had obtained possession of the estate he gave a lease of the Mains to Captain David Ross of Little Daan near Edderton who had served in Lord Strathnaver's Regiment and acted as the Earl's factor between 1720 and 1724. Ross did not live at Skelbo but "maintained 4 men in the house for its defence"[4]. After the estate had been sequestrated the Mains was tenanted firstly by Sir John Gordon of Embo and then by the sub-factor, William Sutherland of Thomskill who lived in the house. There were various pendicles in the Mains, including "The officers possession" for the ground officer or officer for the barony and the "Miln and Croft". Eric Sutherland, Lord Duffus, took over the Mains and house in 1738 and despite accumulating considerable rent arrears was allowed to retain possession until 1760 when William Sutherland of Sciberscross became tacksman[5].

An idea of the layout of the buildings at Skelbo in the late eighteenth century may be obtained from Fig. 1 which is based on an estate survey made by David Aitken in 1788. The house, which dates from the early seventeenth century, is set within the confines of a late medieval castle comprising hall-tower and curtain-wall, a structure which probably replaced an even earlier timber keep or tower on an earthen mound or motte. The ground floor of the house contained two vaulted cellars which were probably used for housing stock and storage. The living quarters were situated on the first floor, to which access was gained by an external stair, and attic. Both first floor and attic were apparently divided into three appartments. The house at Skelbo may be considered to be a northern example of the fortified farmhouses known as bastles which were common in the Borders and which are now being discovered elsewhere in Scotland[6]. It is probable that there were similar houses elsewhere in the Highlands.

The accounts are given in detail; firstly, to assist in the interpretation of this important building and, secondly, to contribute to the identification of builders and their works in the Northern Highlands. Original spellings have been retained but certain contractions have been spelt out in full. Explanations have been placed within square brackets. Some of the accounts are reckoned in £ Scots: during this period the Scottish £ was worth one-twelfth of the £ Sterling. In Sutherland the change-over to Sterling took place between 1730 and 1760.

THE BUILDING ACCOUNTS

Between 1727 and 1728 various repairs were made to the mansion on the orders of Sutherland of Thomskill. On 17 February 1727 Alexander Watson, mason, was paid £3 12 0 (Scots) for "repaireing and helping the Stare which was like to fall and bigging backs for four chimney and helping an window being five days work"[7]. The same day an account was settled with Benjamin Bethune, glazier in Dornoch[8]:

To sixteen Losons [lozenges] put to the windows
in the wester room with new lead and latshadgs
at 2s 6d each loson

	2	0	0
To two losons in the other window ther	0	4	0

To 2 new windows Made for the low Casements
in the said Room both Consisting of eight
foot 6s each foot

	2	8	0

To two more made for the Casments in the

said Room 4 foot each	2	8	0
To ane new window made for the Closet of five foot	1	10	0

To 10 losons put in one of the large windows
in the Dineing-room with new lead & latchets

	1	5	0

To two losons put in the other window there	0	5	0
To Sevin losons put in one of the Casments of the Dineing room	0	14	0
To two Casments Made up for the other window there with sixten losons and new latchets	1	12	0
To the back window in the Dineing room repaired with 18 losins new lead and lachets	1	16	0
To a Casment window repaired in my Lords room with 6 losons and new latcheds	0	12	0
To four losons put in the other window ther	0	10	0
To another Loson put in that room	0	2	0
To a new window made up for the East room of 7 foot	2	5	0
To a loson put in the other window in that room	0	2	0
To a new window put in your Kitchin of 13 foots	3	18	0
To ane weir tirlies [trellis] to the forsaid of 18 foots	4	10	0
To a large shass [sash] loson with new lead put in your Closet	0	6	0
Summa (Scots)	26	7	0

In the summer of that year two slaters, John Ross and James Duncan, were employed to point the house. Their account comprised[9]:

11 roods @ £3 Scot	33	0	0
their Mantenance for 3 Wiekis att 6 Shil: Ster per wiek	10	16	0
To a Borow man for their above 3 wiekes att 6 shil Scots per diem	6	0	0

In the meantime James Mackenzie, smith in Dornoch, had been attending to the door-locks and window catches in the house[10]:

	£	s	d
To makeing six stock looks at one half crown each is	9	0	0
To four Chack looks [check-locks] & five sneks for doors is	8	14	0
To two pair bands for doors	1	16	0
To ane look and ane pair of bands for a press	0	12	0
To ane kie for a press & ane hand & lifter for			

the entrie door	0	12	0
To helping the look & kie of the entrie door	0	12	0
To helping the look of the yeard door	0	6	0
To makeing 3 pair bands for the Garrat windows	0	12	0
To ane Gann of shoos [set of horse shoes]	1	0	0
Summa	23	4	0
Received by me of the above acount	9	12	0
It ane Gad [bar] of Iron weighting ane Stone 12 pound is	3	13	0
It one half boll meal	3	0	0
Received	16	5	0
Remaing restand (Scots)	6	19	0

Between June and August 1728 George Ogilvie and Robert Clark, masons from Coxtoun, near Dunrobin, and James Duncan carried out further work on the house and farm offices[11]:

to three Rood and one quarter New bigged in two Barnes and one Byre att Eight lib Scottes and one boll meal the Rood	26	0	0	3	1	0 0
To one quarter Rood More New bigged in the back off the Wiast barn	2	0	0	0	1	0 0
To the Pinning and harling off three Roods off the old work that stood all two lib Scotes and one firlote meal the Rood is	6	0	0	0	3	0 0
To the harling and Pinning the whole back off the house off Skelbo being five Roodes and a half all two lib Scotes and one firlote Meall per Rood is	11	0	0	1	1	0 0
To the pointing off the Girnell by James Duncan being four Roodes all three lib Scotes and two Peckes the Rood	12	0	0	0	2	0 0
(Scots)	57	0	0	6	0	0 0

The repairs which were made in 1727 and 1728 also required £17 7 0 (Scots) worth of nails, supplied by James Weir[12], and Adam Mackay, slater, was paid £9 4 0 (Scots) "for winning and drawing

900 scleats"[13]. In May 1733 Clark , then described as mason in Golspie, was paid for various work to the girnal or "Grenarie of Skelbo":

pinning and Harleing of the walls of the Girnall upon the mains of Skelbo	£6 (Scots)
winning and dressing of Sclate for, and pointing of the haill rooff of the sd. Girnall	£12 (Scots)

Although Eric Sutherland, Lord Duffus, obtained the Court of Session's permission to spend £80 Sterling on repairs after he became factor in 1735, it does not appear that any work was carried out until ten years' later. In a court action in 1750 Lord Duffus claimed to have spent £37 11 9 on repairs to the buildings at Skelbo including £18 5 8 "in repairing the Mansion house and Garden of Skelbo and building two pillars or Supporters on the outside of the back wall without which the whole must have fallen to the Ground". However, a list of the documents produced in court suggests that between 1745 and 1748 Lord Duffus spent a total of £51 19 6 on the buildings:

Alexander Paterson, mason, for "work wrought at Skelbo", £133 8 0 (Scots)

Donald Junor, mason in Tain, for "work at Skelbo", £176 16 0 (Scots)

Alexander Maccaull, smith in Dornoch, for "Iron Work to the Mansion house and office house", £2 10 6

Walter McCulloch, wright in Dornoch, for "repairing the house of Skelbo", £8 5 0

Donald Duren, slater in Wick, for "mending the Roof of the house", £2 15 0 and for "mending the Roof of the Girnel house", £0 8 0

Adam Mackay in Dornoch, slates for the house, £0 8 0

"Expences of furnishing the Pinners to the office houses", £2 12 0; "of leading Clay and Stones to the office houses", £5 5 0; and "Lime furnished at different times for repairing the office houses", £3 19 0[15].

Further repairs were made by Lord Duffus in 1753 and 1754 for which he was given credit when settling his rents for the Mains. Accounts were submitted for £20 0 10 expended on repairs to the mansion house and girnal in 1753 and for £9 8 2 for work carried out by Alexander Mackay, wright in Achmore?, £8 1 10 for William Junor, mason in Dornoch, and £22 8 0 paid to William Munro, mason, during the financial year 1753-54[16].

In December 1760 the new factor, Gilchrist, informed John Mackenzie, the Earl of Sutherland's legal agent, that an inspection by tradesmen had found the farm buildings to be in "Bad repair" and "no Corn could be safely kept in either Barns or Grannary being in a Ruinous Condition". Moreover by the "excessive high wind" on the 25 December "the Roof & part of the walls of the Girnell is fallen & the other houses much damaged". The new tacksman, William Sutherland of Scibberscross, was suffering and Gilchrist thought that it was a good time to obtain a warrant from the Court to carry out repairs[17].   In July 1761 he reported that the Earl was "senseible" the buildings were "in a very bad condition & not in Skiberscross's power to put them in tollerable Condition for preserving the Corne & Cattle this Season"[18]. It was unreasonable to expect the tacksman to pay for any repairs when he had no lease, "nor can he have any on the footing that Estate is at present".   In the event the Earl advanced Scibberscross £100. Two years later Gilchrist again suggested that an approach be made to the Court but Mackenzie advised against any such move[19].

Between 1760 and 1765 Scibberscross spent £104 11 4 on repairs to the house and office houses[20]:

1760 William Munro, mason	2	19	5
1761 Alexander Mackay, wright	24	13	10
John Mitchell, mason	5	10	4
Angus Sutherland, timber merchant	7	19	3
1762 John Mitchell, mason	2	10	9
William Munro, mason	2	16	0
1763 Alexander Mackay, wright	8	1	8
Alexander Sutherland, timber merchant	2	2	6
William Munro	7	6	5
1764 Alexander Mackay, wright	3	17	6
Simon Ross of Gladfield, timber merchant	8	10	0
1765 William Munro, mason	3	7	6
William Munro, mason	6	18	10
Alexander Mackay, wright	9	3	8
"Boat freight from Bona to Skelbo 2 times	2	4	0
Alexander Mackays expence 2 times	0	10	0
Adition...particulars of which do not appear"	6	0	0
	104	11	8

Matters were eventually to be put on a much firmer footing. New estimates of the further repairs deemed necessary were made in January 1768 by William McBeath, house carpenter at Cambusavie and Alexander Mackay, house carpenter at the Meikle Ferry[21]. Gilchrist and William Sutherland of Sciberscross then petitioned the Court firstly to refund the money which had been expended by Sciberscross and, secondly, as the roof of the mansion had "become so ruinous & decayed, That it must soon fall to the ground, unless it is immediately repaired" to authorise further repairs to be carried out. The mill was in a delapidated state but the mansion was "extremely dangerous for the Tacksman to inhabit it any longer". In August 1769 the Court allowed the factor to spend £84 1 7 on a new roof for the mansion and £18 3 8 on rebuilding the mill[22].

Timber for the roof was purchased in 1770 and work began in the following summer. The task turned out to be much more than had been anticipated for as the Court was later informed, "The wood part of the Roof was so Rotten that how soon an Attempt was made to take it down, the whole tumbled in, and destroyed all the Ceilings and on Examination the whole back wall of the house which had long been propped on Removing the Buttresses, was discovered to be altogether faulty, which was also found to be the case of a great part of both the Extreme Gavels [gables] as well as of the two Midd-Gavels, and the Consequence was that there was an absolute necessity of Rebuilding the whole back wall from the foundation and a great part both of the Extreme and Mid Gavels". James Paterson, mason from Cadboll in Ross-shire who had worked with Alexander Watson, mason from "Drimmy" (Drummuie?) in the parish of Golspie, declared that he had been "employed to Slap [take out] and make up what was unsufficient of the House of Skelbo" and had "found that the North wall had given way by reason of a bad foundation". James Boog, house carpenter at Golspie who was involved in building and repairing many houses, churches and manses in Sutherland and also Ross and Cromarty, stated that the old roof was "in a most Ruinous shattered Condition". It was pointed out that "Daily Experience" taught that "few things eventually turn out more fallacious in point of Expence than the Reparation of an old house"[23].

The accounts submitted by Patterson and Boog indicate the

extensive nature of the building work - indeed parts of the house were rebuilt rather than just repaired. Patterson's account, which was certified by Boog, was settled on 28 February 1772[24]:

To James Pattersons time Employed at the underminding of the back wall being 4 Feet thick viz from May 28th till June 12th which is 13 working days @ 2s per Day	£1	6	0
To Alexr Watson Mason @ Ditto 7 working Days 1s 4d per Day	0	9	4
To Alexr Dallas Ditto at Ditto 6 working Days at Ditto	0	8	0

	[ft ins]
To the length of the back wall including 2 foot for Aditional work to the two Extreme Gables	73 0
by the hight of the side wall	20 5
	1490 5
To the Aditional hight of the fore wall	2 4
by the Lingth	64 6
	150 6
To a mid Gable & Chimnie head	448 0
To a Door Clos'd up with stone & lime in the East Room Gable	6 6
	3 0
	19 6
To a large Window Clos'd up in the East wall	7 4
by	4 6
	52 6
To Altering the Pet stones of 3 Sques	36 0
by	2 4
	84 0
To the Measurment of a Low Vent in the Mid Room Gable	26 0
by	3 3
	84 6
To the Measurment of a Garrat Vent in Ditto	16 0
3 3	52 0
5	

To the Above measurment amounting to

7 Rood 12 yards at £1 15 per Rood	£12	16	8
To Pining & harling the fore wall north Gable & 3 Chimnie heads being 5 Roods 6 yards at 4s 6d per Rood	1	3	3
To a Masson 7 Days hewing & rehewing the old hewn work at 16d per Day	0	8	8
To Aneas Ross Masson the 20th 22nd & 23rd July pinning & making up the Breatches of the inside of fore wall	0	3	0
To Alexr Watson Masson 22nd making up a Britch in the North Gable at 16d per Day James Paterson 22nd at Ditto inside Scunsian [scuncheon] Breatches	0	3	4
To Alexr Dollas Masson 3 Days & John Anderson 3 Days & a Pinnar 6 Days putting a Vent & Chimnie in the North Gable	0	10	6
To a Masson sent from Golspy to cut out bridle holes	0	1	6
To 25 Days work by Donald Mckay Masson for beam filling sloping out one window laying hearth Stones & making Bridle holes in the North Gable	1	5	0
To James Mckinzie Pinner 18 Days work with the said Donald Mackay	0	6	0
To Accompt Paid to Day labourers at taking down the back wall & Cleaning out the Foundation thereof removing the Rubbish & Picking out the Stones from large lumps of the wall throwen dowen	3	11	0
	22	12	3

Patterson was also responsible for making a "sketch or plan of a stair to the House of Skelbo", elsewhere referred to as the "Outter stair of Mason work with stone parapet" and estimated at £5 "if properly finished with correcting of the steps &c"[25]. Boog's account included both "House Carpenter work" and "Glass Locks & hinges"[26]:

To tacking down the old Roof of the House & of an old House at the end of the Main House & rising an old floor	£0	15	0
To Prepairing laying & leaveling the Joists	0	12	0
To Framing & setting up 29 Cupples at 1s 4d Each	1	18	8
To Prepairing & Putting on walplats Rafter feet & Eave boards	0	10	0

To putting on all the Sarking	1	8	0
To prepairing & putting Sleepers in 3 Gables	0	3	0
To making a Sawpit 2s & a Wrights Bench 2s 6d	0	4	6
To prepairing & laying 110 yards flooring at 5d Each	2	5	10
To making 3 Ladders 10 foot Each at 1 d per foot	0	3	9
To Sawing 700 foot for Joisting & Roof at 2s 6d Each	0	17	6
To making 2 Stone barrows 1s 6d Each	0	3	0
To making Rungs & repairing a long Laddar	0	1	6
To making frames for 5 windows at 3s Each	0	15	0
To making a new Window for the Stair Case	0	5	0
To making boxes & borders for 2 hearth Stons	0	4	0
To making & hinging 3 Pannald Doors the Stiles [uprights] of which being cut out of the best of the old Timber 6s Each	0	18	0
To making & setting up 8 Door frames at 1s Each	0	8	0
To making a 9 lighted Window for the Garrat	0	4	6
To prepairing & laying Short Joists & repairing the floor of the East Room with old Timber	0	10	0
To Ditto in the Dining Room & mid Room	0	14	0
To prepairing & setting up 84 yards of Partitioning the Standards being all made of old Timber & all bored & Runged for Cat & Clay Partitions at 4d per yard	1	8	0
To Preparing & setting up the Stairs & hand rail	2	0	0
To making & hinging two new Doors for the Garrats	0	3	0
To fitting & hinging an old Door on the mid Garrat	0	1	0
To cutting the Outter Door in two & hinging it on each side as it hung too much in the Passage in one leaf	0	1	6
To making & hinging a Door on the Cellar below Stairs	0	1	6
To fitting & hinging a Door in the Dining Room as you go to the west Room	0	1	0
To 68 yards of Window & Door facings @ 2d Each	0	11	4
To making hods Trouchs [troughs] Tracles [trestles] & Gangways for the Massons & Scafolding for the Slatters &c.	1	1	0
	£189	7	

Accompt of Glass Locks & hinges for the House of Skelbo

To 4 Squars of Crown Glass for Skie lights Viz			
one at 2s 6d one at 2s & 2 at 1s 3d Each	£0	7	0
To 4 lib Puttie for Ditto at 5d Each	0	1	8
To 12 Squars Glass for Staircase Window 6d Each	0	6	0
To 100 Sprigs [tin wedges] for window frames 4d			
& 3 lib Glue at 1s Each	0	3	4
To 1200 Double Double nails at 1s 4d per 100	0	16	0
To 100 Single Blind nails for Door facings	0	0	6
To 5 Brass handled Door Locks at 5s Each	1	5	0
To 3 Pair Door hinges with Screws at 1s 8d Each	0	5	0
To 9 Squars Glass for Garrat window 7d Each	0	5	3
To 2 large Squars at 9d Each	0	1	6
To 3 Ditto at 7 d Each	0	1	10
To one Pair hinges for Garrat Window	0	1	0
To 2 Sqrs. Glass with puttie 9d Each	0	1	6
To Timber found for the handrail of Stair	0	4	0
	£3	19	7

The account for £22 9 2 was settled by Gilchrist on 6 July, 1772. The account submitted by William Ross, slater at New Tarbat, had already been paid on 17 December 1771[27]:

	£	Sh	d
To tirring [stripping the roof of] the house of			
Skelbo Containing Seven Roods @ 3 Sh per Rood	1	1	0
To Sclating the said Roof Containing Seven Roods			
at 16s 8d per Rood	5	16	8
To four Panes in Said Roof	0	4	0
To Two Stone of Hair for said Work at 1s 8d per			
Stone	0	3	4
	7	5	0

In July 1772 Boog drew up a detailed estimate of the work, particularly "Plaister work", required to finish the house[28]:

Dining Room

	£		
To 48 yards Cilling Plaister at 6d Each	£ 1	4	0
To leaveling the Roof of Ditto for the Lath	0	7	0
To 25 Ten foot flooring Dales for Lath &			
Cleats for the Joists	1	5	0
To Sawing 48 Draughts for Lath 2d Each	0	8	0
To 92 yards Stone wall Plaister 2d Each	0	15	4

	£	s	d
To 3000 Lath nails 2s per 1000	0	6	0
To 20 Bols Lime at 1s Each	1	0	0
To 30 yards washing boards 2d Each	0	5	0
	£ 5	10	4

Mid Room

	£	s	d
To 24 yards Cilling Plaister at 6d each	£ 0	12	0
To Leaveling the Roof for the lathing	0	3	6
To 13 ten foot flooring Dales for lath Cleats & washing boards	0	13	0
To Sawing 24 Draughts for Lath 2d Each	0	4	0
To 64 yards Stone wall plaister at 2d Each	0	10	8
To 1500 Lath nails for the Roof	0	3	0
To 20 yards washing boards 2d Each	0	3	4
To 14 Bols lime for Ditto	0	14	0
	£ 3	3	6

East Room

	£	s	d
To 28 yards Cilling Plaister at 6d Each	£ 0	14	0
To Leaveling the Roof for the Lath	0	4	0
To 15 flooring Dales for Ditto	0	15	0
To Sawing 26 Draughts for Lath 2d Each	0	4	4
To 69 yards Stonwall Plaister 2d Each	0	11	6
To 2000 Lath nails	0	4	0
To 22 yards washing boards 2d Each	0	3	8
To 15 Bols lime for Ditto	0	15	0
	£ 3	11	6

Passage

	£	s	d
To 11 yards Cilling Plaister 6d Each	£ 0	5	6
To leaveling the Joists for Ditto	0	1	8
To 6 flooring Dales 1s Each	0	6	0
To Sawing 12 Draughts 2d Each	0	2	0
To 48 yards Ston wall Plaister 2d Each	0	8	0
To 1000 Lath nail	0	2	0
To 7 Bols lime for Ditto	0	7	0
	£ 1	12	2

Stair Case

	£	s	d
To 30 yards Stone wall Plaister 2d Each	£ 0	5	0
To 9 yards Cilling Ditto 6d Each	0	4	6
To 6 Dales for Ditto 1s Each	0	6	0
To Sawing 10 Draughts 2d Each	0	1	8

To 500 Lath nails	0	1	0
To 6 Bols lime	0	6	0
To leaveling the Cuples for Lathing	0	1	6
£	1	5	8

Mid Garrat Room

To 20 yards Cilling Plaister at 6d Each	£0	10	0
To leaveling the Cuples for the lathing	0	4	0
To 12 Dales for Ditto	0	12	0
To Sawing 20 Draughts at 2d Each	0	3	4
To 26 yards Stone wall plaister 2d Each	0	4	4
To 1500 Lath nails	0	3	0
To 12 Bols lime	0	12	0
£2	8	8

East Garrat Room

To 38 yards Cilling Plaister 6d Each	£0	19	0
To 20 Dales for Lath	1	0	0
To leaveling the Roof	0	6	0
To Sawing 30 Draughts 2d Each	0	5	0
To 20 yards Stone wall plaister 2d each	0	3	4
To 2000 lath nails	0	4	0
To 14 Bols lime	0	14	0
£ 3	11	4

Shutters for 5 Windows

To 15 Dales at 1s Each	0	15	0
To making & hinging 5 Pair Shutters at 4s Each	1	0	0
To 10 Pair hinges with Screws 1s Each	0	10	0
£	2	5	0
in all	£	23	8	2

Golspy Tower 6th July 1772
This is the Estimate of the Plaister work &c. which is
nececary to be made up in the House of Skelbo which is
computed to the best of my Skill & amountes to Twenty three
Pound Eight Shillings & two Pence Sterling to which is to be
added five Shillings Sterling for my Trouble in going to
Skelbo & measuring the Masson & Slatter work being sent there
two Different times & thus Estimate is Certifyed by James
Boog

This work was probably executed after a second warrant had been obtained from the Court in March 1773. The account was paid by Gilchrist in September 1775[29]:

To 48 yards Cilling Plaister in Dining Room 6d each	£1	4	0
To leaveling the Roof of Ditto for lathing	0	7	0
To 26 Deals for Lath & Clates at 1s Each	1	6	0
To Sawing 48 Draughts for Lath 2d Each	0	8	0
To 92 yards Stone wall plaister 2d Each	0	15	4
To 3000 Lath nails 2s Each	0	6	0
To 30 yards washing boards 2d Each	0	5	0
	£ 4	11	4

Mid Room of Midflat

To 24 yards Cilling Plaister 6d Each	£ 0	12	0
To leaveling the Roof for Lathing	0	3	6
To 16 Deals for Lath Clates & washing boards	0	16	0
To Sawing 24 Draughts for Lath 2d Each	0	4	0
To 64 yards Stone wall plaister 2d Each	0	10	8
To 1,500 Lath nails for the Roof 2s	0	3	0
To 20 yards washing boards 2d Each	0	3	4
	£ 2	12	6

East Room Midflat

To 28 yards Cilling Plaister @ 6d Each	0	14	0
To leaveling the Roof for Lathing	0	4	0
To 15 Deals for Lath &c.	0	15	0
To Sawing 26 Draughts for Lath 2d Each	0	4	4
To 69 yards Stone wall Plaister 2d Each	0	11	6
To 2,000 Lath nails	0	4	0
To 22 yards washing boards 2d Each	0	3	8
	2	16	6

Passage Midflat

To 11 yards Cilling Plaister 6d Each	£ 0	5	6
To leaveling the Joists for Ditto	0	1	8
To 9 flooring Deals for Lath &c 1s	0	9	0
To Sawing 12 Draughts at 2d Each	0	2	0
To 48 yards Stone wall Plaister 2d ea	0	8	0
To 1,000 Lath nails	0	2	0
	1	8	2

Stair Case

To 30 yards Stone wall Plaister 2d Each	0	5	0
To 9 yards Cilling Ditto 6d	0	4	6
To 7 Deals for Lath &c 1s Each	0	7	0
To Sawing 10 Draughts 2d Each	0	1	8
To 500 Lath nails	0	1	0
To Leaveling the Cuples for Lathing	0	1	6
	1	0	8

East Garrat Room

To 38 yards Cilling Plaister 6d Each	£	0	19	0
To 26 Deals for Lath 1s Each		1	6	0
To leaveling the Roof		0	6	0
To Sawing 30 Draughts 2d Each		0	5	0
To 20 yards Stone wall Plaister 2d Each		0	3	4
To 2000 Lath nails		0	4	0
		3	3	4

To Matts. making & hinging 4 Pair Shutters @ 9 Shs. Each	1	16	0
To Measuring the Masson & Slatters works of the House of Skelbow	0	5	0
To Cash Paid Labs. for Ridling watering Sowering & working the Lime	1	10	0
To 3 Stone nolt hair 2s Each	0	6	0
To 600 Double nails 8d Each	0	4	0
To 200 Double Double	0	2	8
	4	3	8
	19	16	2

Golspy Tower September 30th 1775 Received from
Dugald Gilchrist Esqr Factor for the estate of
Skilbo Payment of the above Accompt of nineteen
Pound Sixteen Shillings & two Pence Sterling & the
same is Discharged by me   James Boog

N.B. there was 77 Bols lime used for the Plaister work of Each	3	17	0
	23	13	2

The timber for the house had been bought from Hugh Falconer, a
merchant in Inverness, and was shipped over in two cargoes from

Lovat by John Cuthbert, skipper in Inverness. The first cargo, delivered on 7 August 1770 comprised[30]:

To 37 Pieces square Fir Timber measureing 170 solid feet at 8d: each peice haveing the length thereof & the solid contents mark'd on it with a Coopers iron	5	13 8
13 Dozin Deals 1) inches thick & 10 feet long @ 10s	6	10 0
15 Dozin Ditto . Ditto & 10 feet long at 6s	4	10 0
	£ 16	13 8

The second cargo, delivered on 15 August, comprised:

To 32 pieces square Timber 136 solid feet at 8d each piece marked as above	4	10 8
13 Dozin & 8 Deals 1 inch thick 10 feet long at 10s	6	16 8
15 Dozin Deals . inch thick & 10 feet long at 6s	4	10 0
	£ 15	17 4

Shipping costs amounted to £5 3 0[31]. The account for lime whch was supplied by the tacksman, William Sutherland, was settled on 28 February 1772[32]:

To 273 bolls lime for the Rubble work		
To 12 bolls for pinning and harling		
To 10 Bolls for a vent & Breaches within the house		
To 10 bolls for beam filling &c		
To 10 bolls laid in harling the inside of the old work kept up		
315		
To the Expence or price of the @ 315 at one Shil. per Boll	£ 15	15 0
To the Expence of drawing 229 bolls of Sand at the rate of 15 bolls per day being 1 Shil each horse per day at 3 firlots to the boll lime	0	15 0
	£ 16	10 0

4500 "Easdale Slates" at 37/- per 1000 were shipped from Findhorn to Brora and from there to Skelbo by William Forsyth in Cromarty. The total cost, including £1 2 2 for freight, was £9 8 8[33]. 49 pound of "lump lead" and 75 fathoms of rope was supplied by John Duncan, merchant in Dornoch, at a cost of £1 4 9[34]. With the exception of those bought from Montgomery, most of the nails came from Dunrobin[35]:

5200 double Naills @ 5/-	1	6	0
4800 blind flooring 5/-	1	4	0
7400 Slate Nails 5/-	1	17	0
256 Spikes at 3/6 per 100		9	0
100 lath Naills at 2/			3
3000 Slate Naills from John Montgomry at			
New tarbat	1	2	0
	5	18	3

The legal costs incurred in obtaining the two warrants from the court amounted to a further £20 13 12[36].

SUMMARY

Between 1723 and 1787 over £400 was expended on repairs to the house and farm buildings at Skelbo:

1727-28	18	0	10
1733	1	10	0
1745-48	51	19	6
1753-54	59	18	10
1760-65	104	11	8
1771-73	172	8	6
	£408	9	4

This expenditure must be set against a total estate rental of about £450 per annum at the commencement of the sequestration in 1723. However, the collectable rent, that is the rent of the lands which were not wadsetted out, only amounted to between £200-270, depending upon the price of grain. It was only after 1774 that the Skelbo estate realised a rent of £620-760[37].

It is evident that, despite the contraints imposed by the sequestration, efforts were made to maintain the property in good order. Apart from the restoration of the house of Skelbo, it is apparent that other buildings on the estate were repaired, such as the "mansion" of Blairich in 1784, tenants were found for waste lands, and the development of new settlements and tenancies was actively encouraged. In 1772 Boog declared that the work on the house of Skelbo had "been done so Effectually that it is now equal to a new House and is a very Comfortable habitation"[58]. Some 17 years later, after Sciberscross had died, the new owners of the estate, the Sutherland family, gave Boog a liferent possession of his "very Comfortable habitation".

ACKNOWLEDGEMENTS

The author would like to thank the Countess of Sutherland for kindly giving permission to quote from the Sutherland Papers, the staff of the National Library of Scotland for their courteous assistance, Dr Annette Smith for arranging access to the Forfeited Estates Papers and Geoffrey Stell for providing material on the architecture of Skelbo.

REFERENCES

1 The repairs to the mill of Skelbo will be treated in an article devoted to eighteenth-century Sutherland mills.
2. G. Stell "Architecture and Society in Easter Ross before 1707" in J.R. Baldwin (ed.) *Firthlands of Ross and Sutherland* (1986) p.101.
3. The history of the Skelbo estate in the seventeenth and eighteenth centuries will be examined at more length elsewhere.
4. National Library of Scotland (hereafter NLS) Dep. 313/564 D. Ross to the Earl of Sutherland, 17 October 1724, 3129 Accompt Sir Tho: Calder; Scottish Record Office (hereafter SRO) SC9/7/10 Process Lord Duffus agt Wm Ross.
5. NLS MS1483, 159; Dep. 313/3129 L. Brodie to Sir T. Calder, 23 June 1727, 3134 Rectiefied state of the process . . . 1738; SRO SC9/7/8 Decreet James Mclean v Erick Sutherland.
6. RCHME (1970) Shielings and Bastles; T. Ward "The Elusive Scottish Bastle House" *Vernacular Building* (1988) p.12.
7. NLS Dep. 313/3133 Accompt Allexr Watson measson.
8. NLS Dep. 313/3133 discharged accompt Beatone Glazior To Sutherland.
9. NLS Dep. 313/3133 Dischargd account Sclatteres.
10. NLS Dep. 313/3133 discharged account Ja: Mackenzie.
11. NLS Dep. 313/3133 discharged account for Meason work...
12. NLS Dep. 313/3133 Disscharged Accot for Nails.

13. NLS Dep. 313/3129 Accompt Sir Tho: Calder.
14. NLS Dep. 313/3133 Robt Clerks receipt.
15. SRO SC9/7/8 Decreet James McLean v Erick Sutherland.
16. SRO GD153 Box 48 Note of Payments By Lord Duffus of Rents of Skelbo, [Account], Account of Capernochs Intromissions ...1743...51, Accot of Capernochs Intromissions...1751...1755.
17. NLS MS1484, 3.
18. NLS MS1484, 25.
19. NLS MS1484, 151 and 222; Dep. 313/1097, 4.
20. NLS Dep. 313/1724 State of the Expence...
21. NLS Dep. 313/1724 State of the Expence...
22. NLS Dep. 313/1724 Act and Warrand In favours of Gilchrist and Sutherland 1769. See also SRO CS103/92.
23. NLS Dep. 313/1724 Act and Warrant In favours of Dugald Gilchrist 1773. For Boog see Sage, D. (1899) *Memorabilia Domestica*, 121-122; a list of the projects with which he was involved is in the course of preparation.
24. NLS Dep. 313/1724 Dischd. Accot. James Paterson.
25. NLS Dep. 313/1724 Act and Warrant...1773.
26. NLS Dep. 313/1724 House Carpenters Accot.
27. NLS Dep. 313/1724 Accot pd Wm Ross Slatter.
28. NLS Dep. 313/1724 Estimate of Plaister &c.
29. NLS Dep. 313/1724 Dischd Accot James Boog.
30. NLS Dep. 313/1722 Mr Falconnars Discharged Accot of Timber.
31. NLS Dep. 313/1724 [Cuthbert's receipt].
32. NLS Dep. 313/1724 Rect for Lime &c.
33. NLS Dep. 313/1724 Wm Forsyth.
34. NLS Dep. 313/1724 Duncan.
35. NLS Dep. 313/1724 State of the Expence..., Nails.
36. NLS Dep. 313/1724 State of the Expence.
37. NLS Dep. 313/3132 Account of Rental of Skelbo...1737; SRO CS96/3225; Forfeited Estates Papers: Rentall of the Estate of Kenneth late Lord Duffus (these papers are presently being catalogued at the University of St. Andrews).
38. NLS Dep. 313/1724 Act and Warrant...1773.